Postwar Casualty
Canada's Merchant Navy

Doug Fraser

Pottersfield Press
Lawrencetown Beach
Nova Scotia

© 1997 William Douglas Fraser

All rights reserved. No part of this publication may be reproduced or transmitted in any form or by any means, electronic or mechanical, including photocopying, or by any information storage or retrieval system, without permission in writing from the publisher.

Canadian Cataloguing in Publication Data

Fraser, Doug, 1920–

Postwar Casualty

ISBN 1–895900–07–7

1. Merchant marine — Canada — History — 20th century. 2. World War, 1939–1945 — Campaigns — Atlantic Ocean. 3. World War, 1939–1945 — Transportation. 4. Fraser, Doug, 1920– 5. World War, 1939–1945 — Personal narratives, Canadian. I. Title.

D810.T8F72 1997   940.54'5971   C97–950024–9

Pottersfield Press gratefully acknowledges the ongoing support of the Nova Scotia Department of Education, Cultural Affairs Division, as well as the Canada Council and the Department of Canadian Heritage.

Printed and bound in Canada

Pottersfield Press
Lawrencetown Beach
83 Leslie Road, East Lawrencetown
Nova Scotia, Canada, B2Z 1P8

Contents

Acknowledgements	7
Foreword	9
Introduction	11
Call to war	15
Prejudice then, prejudice now	27
Home port, old city	39
Ships – Convoys – Casualties	51
Recognition – Vanishing dream	67
Halifax, May 7, 1945	79
Death of a leader	89
Yesterday's children	103
Politics pervades	111
Pay and income tax	120
Post-war pariahs	129
The last hurrah	142

To Blanche

Acknowledgements

I deeply appreciate the encouragement of those who helped with advice, information, and recounted their own personal experiences. I take full responsibility for errors, omissions and opinions.

My thanks to Bud Doucette of Toronto, president of the Canadian Merchant Navy Veterans Association, and to the memory of his predecessor, the late Tom McGrath of Vancouver. Also to Don Tremain, OC, of Halifax, who read the first draft of the book and helped with advice on historical details; he is a scholar of wartime history.

Two master mariners, Ken Moore and John Samson of Halifax were most generous with their advice and guidance. And a very special thank-you to Russ Latimer of Dartmouth, NS, chronicler of marine adventure, of ships and those who sailed them, and fellow member of the Society of Wireless Pioneers.

Doug Fraser

Foreword

This book has been written as a personal commentary and response to half a century of neglect of Canadians who served at sea during the Second World War as merchant mariners.

Federal governments have consistently refused to recognize them as veterans. At war's end they were not provided with rehabilitation benefits or educational programs at technical trades, or in colleges. The federal civil service would not interview them for employment because that privilege had been reserved for veterans of the armed forces, whether they had served in a war zone or not.

Fifty years after the end of the Second World War, merchant seamen still alive, and the widows of the deceased, received the Canadian Voluntary Service Medal.

It is not a pleasant history and the heedless attitude of a succession of parliaments continues and worse still, with inaccurate claims by cabinet ministers that full veteran status has been granted to merchant marine veterans. The refusal to grant them similar status to veterans of the armed forces continues with the concurrence of the Royal Canadian Legion, the National Council of Veterans Associations, the Army, Navy and Air Force Association, and the RCN Association.

Doug Fraser

Introduction

Giving meaning to the tragedy of war and its many consequences is the theme of this enlightening and thought-provoking compendium which skillfully describes the valiant service of all ranks who manned merchant marine vessels in storm and enemy-ravaged waters. It describes the part they played in transporting millions of tons of vitally needed food, petroleum, munitions, and troops, all urgent essentials and paramount to fighting a war.

The risks were heavy; they sailed against daunting odds; one seaman in ten would die by enemy action before the war ended, victims of U-boats attacks and armed raiders. These men met the challenge with honour in the task of carrying precious cargoes across dangerous seas.

Senior naval command repeated the sobering words of Winston Churchill: "The Battle of the Atlantic was not won by our navy or air force; it was won by the courage, fortitude, and determination of Allied merchant seamen."

Many of the dramas of the Second World War, both ashore and afloat, will be found within the pages of this book, relating from a unique perspective, the factual story of the merchant navy's war efforts — an exercise often regarded as a sidelight to important actions of the armed forces.

In a striking way it tells of the tension and constant responsibilities of merchant seamen in facing untold periods of endurance in this, the longest and most demanding and unremitting battle of history, a protracted conflict on global seas. Although classed as the fourth arm of the service, nothing of consequence on the long path to victory could have happened without the delivery of merchant ship cargoes across the wide seas of the globe.

At war's end Canada's merchant seamen accounted for a much higher death-ratio than the armed forces but have gone unnoticed and unappreciated and without deserved recognition for some fifty years. The slow change toward a weak semblance of veteran status has come, not willingly, after years of intense and unproductive negotiations with government authorities.

As a reward for wartime services rendered merchant seamen faced unemployment as the post-war merchant fleet was hastily dispatched into the hands of foreign owners. Participation in war memorials and parades, Remembrance Day services, educational and housing assistance, job preferences, all were non-existent. Negative reward for immeasurable service.

Author Doug Fraser, a native-born Nova Scotian, retired merchant navy officer, successful long-time journalist, and editor of the Merchant Navy Veterans Association newsletter, *The Red Duster*, has compiled a remarkably well detailed and carefully researched overview which has resulted in a genuine, absorbing, and permanent treatise.

Russell F. Latimer

Bedford Basin, Halifax, Nova Scotia, 1941
    Tankers and dry-cargo ships gather in Bedford Basin in preparation for convoy. The day before eighty ships of varied sizes and purpose weighed anchor and proceeded through the Narrows, to the right, and out Halifax harbour to the open sea, destination the United Kingdom.
    In the foreground is the Fairview yards of Canadian National Railways, the staging point for millions of tons of war matériel to be transported across the Atlantic. The railyards now serve Ceres and Halterm, the two container terminals in Halifax. (Photo: Public Archives of Nova Scotia, Bolinger 1941 #460B)

Lady Nelson

Built in 1927 at the Cammell-Laird yards in Birkenhead, UK, from 1928 to 1942, the Lady Nelson was the flagship of the Canadian National Steamship Line, running between Halifax, Nova Scotia and the Caribbean as a passenger liner.

In 1942 she was torpedoed dockside in Castries harbour, St. Lucia. Refloated and towed in damaged condition to Mobile, Alabama, she was converted to Canada's first hospital ship. *Lady Nelson* survived the Second World War, was sold to Egyptian interests in 1952 and renamed the *Gumhuryat Misr* serving as a passenger ship plying Mediterranean ports between Alexandria and Marseilles. In 1960 her name was changed to *Alwadi*. On December 18, 1965 she was docked in Alexandria in a damaged condition and was sold in 1968 for demolition. (Photo: F. Mannington Collection, Maritime Musuem of the Atlantic, No. 8822)

Call to war

From the beginning of hostilities in 1939 through to 1941 Canada's merchant navy consisted of a motley collection of venerable cargo vessels, a number of survivors of earlier times. In years past the Canadian Government Merchant Marine operated to several continents. Tankers ferried petroleum from Venezuelan oil fields to refineries in Montreal and Dartmouth. Almost all of our export trade including newsprint and minerals had been carried in foreign flag bottoms.

Five passenger ships, the pride of our service, were built for the southern trade and honoured with the names of distinguished admirals of the Royal Navy: *Lady Nelson*, *Lady Drake*, *Lady Rodney*, *Lady Hawkins*, and *Lady Somers*. During the 1930s they sustained ocean trade between the islands and Canada, calling at Bermuda, the Bahamas, and Caribbean ports.

After mid-1941, ships available for convoy duty included the commercial fleets from occupied countries which had been at sea or in foreign ports when the Germans moved into their home countries. Norway possessed the world's largest number of commercial carriers, well-built and maintained and carrying highly professional crews from master to deck boy. The hundreds of ships flying the red, white and blue colours of the Norwegian flag were now in the fight against the enemies of their mountain homeland. Refugee ships from many other occupied countries, including Denmark, the

Netherlands, and Greece, were also part of the Allied fleet, paying their own way from cargo fees.

In the gray autumn of 1939 organizers of Canada's war effort invoked the wisdom of hindsight and moved immediately to look for experienced mariners, placing special emphasis on deck and engineer officers and able-bodied seamen. Apparently modest optimism led officials to believe that ships could be bought from other countries or eventually built in Canada, if hostilities continued long enough for shipyards to be organized or expanded. There were problems in that area; it would take time to train fabricators and welders and other workers capable of assembling steel ships. In the meantime, officials searched for potential crews; they hired men who had enough knowledge of marine matters to tell a bowline from a back splice to man a varied collection of ancient tubs to be bought or chartered out of retirement in some distant backwater of the globe. Among them would be flat-bottomed vessels coming downriver from the Great Lakes for a taste of salt water.

Obtaining suitable manpower was somewhat easier for mainly historic and economic reasons. Inshore fishermen in the Maritimes' harbours and coves had become accustomed to bad weather and were instinctive navigators. Those who crewed in Lunenburg schooners to the Grand Banks were bluewater men, as were the Newfoundland sealers who went down north to the ice. Many younger men from what is now the Atlantic provinces were in the navy early on, yet many more in their middle years welcomed a shipping chance. With luck, a man could abandon the life of a hangashore and earn money to send back home.

Cooks and stewards could be hired from among those who had been at sea in the Hungry Thirties and until war began had puttered about unemployed or working in lumber camps. Some younger men and a number of young women trained on their own initiative to become wireless operators, paying their own tuition for night classes with no assistance from government. Some radio operators in training had been rejected by the armed forces for varying disabilities ranging from poor vision to colour blindness to flat feet. One class of fourteen in Ernest Johnson's radio school on Young Street in Halifax reported five of their group lost to enemy action within two years of gaining their certificates of competency.

Ernie Johnson, an Irishman who had served in the Royal Navy for twenty-one years, served in the Battle of Jutland in the 1914-18 war. After retirement, he worked another quarter century for the Marconi Company as a communications specialist. His widow, Mabel, died in a Halifax nursing home in 1994 at the age of 106.

Former seamen returning to the merchant service were considerably older than those with sea experience joining the armed forces, principally the navy. Men in their thirties, forties and fifties were reporting to the shipping office in Halifax and other ports. H.T. Preedy, shipping master at the Halifax office on Granville Street, was a balding gnome of a chap who affected a set of steel-rimmed spectacles although heaven only knew why. Mr. Preedy's cold and modestly bloodshot blue eyes peered over the top of his glasses in a hard look that seemed to penetrate the nervous souls of young seamen, especially the beardless ones joining their first ship.

"Your full name, young man!" It was a challenge not a question. When I responded, he wrote it down in copper-plate in a large journal that had been around since the First World War, perhaps before.

"You're signing on, I presume. The purser was in this morning with your personal details, next of kin, permanent address."

The shipping master removed his superfluous spectacles and wiped his bald head with a handkerchief. "What's your ticket number?"

"5786, sir. I have it right here."

The glasses returned to his wine-red nose. "I'll take your word for it, boy. Now sign the articles here, and take them in the envelope to the purser when you report aboard. Go directly to the Cable Wharf at the foot of George Street. And don't stop off for drink or other mischief."

Old H.T. was much respected by seagoing men in and out of Halifax. He operated as a maritime employment office with unofficial but tacit approval of the Ministry of Transport. Mr. Preedy maintained a list of able seamen, firefighters, stewards, and even some of no trades but seeking four-on and four-off and three meals a day; the Depression still lingered in recent memory. More men than we can ever know got a discreet telephone call from the old chap when a vessel's master or chief officer happened to be looking for hands to replace anyone who had jumped ship or been invalided ashore to the dubious mercies of the sick mariner program. The Halifax shipping master was widely known for his memory of names, faces, and perhaps even the certificate qualifications of every seaman passing through his establishment. A memorial plaque would not be out of place on the wall of the Royal Bank building on George Street, site of the old wooden structure where he observed and expedited the papers of merchant vessels and crews over many years.

Captain John Mackenzie of Pope's Harbour on Nova Scotia's Eastern Shore was a longtime friend of Mr. Preedy. He had been a master mariner for about four decades when the Second World War began, and had captained umrunners, cargo schooners and tramp ships with their coal-fired reciprocating engines. A man from my home village had sailed with him as able seaman in the late 1920s and he described "Old Peg" as a fearless and immensely capable skipper. He earned his nickname the hard way: as a young man he lost a leg to a steel hawser that snapped, performing instant amputation. Demerara rum from the vessel's cargo served as the only after-the-fact painkiller.

Such sturdy seagoing men often could be seen on the narrow streets of the island of St. Pierre, off Newfoundland's Burin Peninsula. The French colony prospered during the prohibition era as a staging platform for rumrunners from Barbados and Demerara. Those cargoes through clandestine delivery eventually found thirsty markets on the east coast of the United States and Canada's Atlantic shores. I first saw Captain Mackenzie in the early 1930s; he performed in an amateur play presented at St. Peter's Hall in Sheet Harbour. A fine natural actor, as I remember, he played the part of a one-legged master mariner, which he certainly was, with considerable insouciance.

Over several years I encountered Captain MacKenzie a number of times, listening to the sea stories and anecdotes stored in his great reserve of memory. He was not the first man to offer the opinion, heard many times since, that shipowners and agents prosper while crews are considered cattle to be fed just enough to stay alive and work. I met him one day on Hollis Street where we stopped for a chat; he was headed toward the CN Telegraph office to wire Omaha for a supply of heavy wool socks he said were necessary to the comfort of his "starboard stump." I still remember him as he looked on that day in 1940, bearded and with wide smile and eyes as blue as the Caribbean.

A year later, his name appeared in newspaper headlines in the United States, Britain, and Canada. He had been master of the American cargo vessel *Pink Star* torpedoed off Iceland, the first United States ship lost to German action in the Second World War. Captain MacKenzie and his crew took to the lifeboats safely. The submarine surfaced and sank the vessel with her deck gun. The *Pink Star* dipped under, the Stars and Stripes on the gaff snapping in the wind. After a British destroyer picked up master and crew, Captain MacKenzie reported to his owners that the ship's cash for crew payment and supplies was safe, wrapped in oiled canvas and stowed in the hollow of his wooden leg.

When war began in 1939 there was apprehension and much speculation on how long hostilities might last. Most people were convinced that democracy would somehow defeat the fascists in short order. Others not so confident realized the immense challenge. From Winston Churchill to the middle-aged survivors of the trenches and men who had lived through long months of submarine warfare in the Atlantic, all were convinced the Axis powers would be defeated but knew it would take years to accomplish with many lives lost. John MacKenzie was prophetic when he commented: "Lads in knee pants now in school will be killed in action before this war is over." As a student of modern history who lived through many of the great or nefarious events of the early twentieth century, he was an intrigued observer of the shifting sands of reality in a Europe still suffering the consequences of the Congress of Vienna and its heritage of the invidious art of diplomacy.

Master mariners are themselves an interesting lot. They are usually serene practitioners of the craft of navigation and instinctively respond to the challenge of far horizons. For those of more inquiring mind there is time to meditate, to broaden general knowledge of the world and its peoples. The management and supervision of other human beings under the autocratic conditions of marine command is a continuing educational process for the mind that is both alert and studious. I was fortunate to encounter a number of these individuals, including a retired commander in the Royal Navy who had been returned to civilian life in 1924 under the cost-saving naval retrenchment program known as the "Geddes Axe," a moniker derived from the narrow-pursed individual whose Scottish heritage may have influenced his compression of the Admiralty budget. Britain was not the only nation to pare down defence spending in the 1920s.

Commander Bredin Delap was one of several hundred naval officers permitted to qualify as master mariners with a Board of Trade certificate. I served under his command for a couple of years before he was invalided ashore and moved to a farm in the Annapolis Valley of Nova Scotia. His successor, Bill Adamson, was the son of a Scottish moulder who served in Ramsay Macdonald's first Labour government in the United Kingdom. Bill's mother, Jennie Laurel Adamson, was a member of Clement Attlee's cabinet in the 1945 Labour government. Captain Adamson was a student of European history, both political and economic, and not far from his socialist father's reformist spirit. As a young man sailing out of

London in the 1920s, he spent his brief shore leaves at hotel parties or dance clubs. One person he met was an American who played saxophone in the Savoy Hotel orchestra. The young musician wasn't a featured singer at the time but Rudy Vallee gained considerable fame in the years ahead.

The many stories of famous or notorious people, of great cities and distant ports stimulated in me a natural curiosity to some day visit exotic places which had only been curious names in my geography book. It was vastly interesting and educational to sail with individuals of rare diversity: one had been apprenticed on a square-rigged ship running wheat from Freemantle, Australia to Liverpool, UK. Another had cargo ship experience on the Coromandel Coast of India, while others engaged in exotic interests ashore in foreign ports from Fortaleza, Brazil to Amsterdam.

Those were the pleasant aspects of serving aboard ship. Yet the knowledge that these were times of hostility on the seas, or rather under the seas, never left our consciousness. The U-boat menace was very real; several of my classmates at the radio school were dead within months of getting their ticket and joining the first ship available. As with those who survived, their desire had involved making use of many months of hard study and applying our modest skills where they might be required. At times the sight of the next sunrise amounted to a matter of luck; misadventure always loomed as a possibility and such thoughts chilled the bones. Events, as they usually do, occur so swiftly that shivers develop after the fact, as happened when the cableship *Cyrus Field* was New York-bound on the last day of the European war.

We cleared the tip of Cape Cod at dawn, only the top of the Pilgrim's Tower in Provincetown visible above the mist lying low over a calm sea as we proceeded southward toward the north canal entrance. We hove to off the Coast Guard Station at the mouth of the waterway and waited for clearance to proceed. The canal was built in the 1930s by the Works Progress Administration, an agency organized early in President Roosevelt's New Deal. Its foresighted concept involved providing employment at modest pay for the jobless and destitute victims of the Great Depression. Shortly after noon we were through the canal with a course set down Buzzard's Bay past Cuttyhunk Island into Long Island Sound. Our destination was New York, west southwest down the Sound through Hell's Gate to the East River then around the Battery and up the Hudson side of Manhattan to the ocean-liner berths at midtown.

The war in Europe being in its last hours, guns remained at rest for the moment, although enemy submarines were still at sea. The U-boat fleet had been ordered by what was left of the German admiralty to proceed immediately toward the nearest Allied port and surrender boat and crew. Most undersea commanders followed instructions. Not so the die-hard-or-die-soon Nazi fanatics and a few commanders who didn't receive the surrender order either through equipment breakdown or transmission interference. New York radio stations were full of war news; official announcement of Germany's surrender was expected at any moment.

U-853 at that moment was proceeding submerged toward the American coast with what might have been the intention of surfacing close to shore and raising the black flag. It is more likely that the twenty-four-year-old commander, Lieutenant Helmut Froemsdorf, intended to keep his options open, surrender as a last resort or torpedo an Allied vessel as a final gesture of defiance. Moving toward the same point on the chart, as if making transit with the submarine, was the American collier *Black Point* bound up-channel toward the Cape Cod Canal with her cargo of 7,700 tons of Virginia coal destined for the Edison plant in south Boston.

As freighter and sub pursued their intersecting courses, our ship the *Cyrus Field* had proceeded off Newport, Rhode Island, in quieter days the summer haunt of the very rich. Off the mouth of Narragansett Bay and abeam of Point Judith, the *Black Point* appeared in the cross-hairs of *U-853* now at shallow depth.

"Feuer!" Froemsdorf snapped. The torpedoman pushed the red button and the steel fish sped toward the coal carrier.

"Whaaammm!" The explosion's shock wave rang our hull plates like a sledge hammer striking an empty oil barrel a yard from my ear. The booming sound wave of the blast that blew apart the after third of the *Black Point* followed a second later, a giant sound painful to the ear drums and moving through the air at half the speed it traversed the water.

Twelve men died, as we heard later, while survivors took to the life-rafts with the collier's radio operator borrowing a hurried moment to send out SSSS, the wartime signal for submarine attack, rather than the peacetime SOS distress signal. When he scrambled toward the raft, the master was waiting for him, determined to be the last man off his doomed vessel. By chance four American destroyers were coning abeam of Block Island. Having escorted an ocean convoy into New York, they were now bound north for Boston. All four immediately began the hunt, chasing down all sonar blips with depth-charge patterns in an operation that would be completed sixteen hours later when the submarine lay blasted open at the bottom of Long Island Sound.

Our vessel had joined others in getting a boat over the side to pick up possible survivors, but other boats had already arrived on the scene, their crews lifting bodies from the water. We saw a number of floating denim hats of the kind worn by deck and engine-room hands; under some rescuers found the life-jacketed bodies of men killed by the explosion and blown over the side. As the sub hunt began shore authorities warned us by coastal radio that further attacks might be forthcoming; no one knew if the current attack had been a solo effort or whether other U-boats were approaching the coast. Allied intelligence had estimated the number of German subs at sea and many of them might be under contingency orders to undertake suicide attacks in the Reich's last gasp. No one had forgotten that a sub commander had machine gunned refugee children in lifeboats after torpedoing the ship carrying them toward east coast ports of North America.

We were ordered to resume course down the sound and maintain full alert, a normal condition that included lifeboat drill for merchant ships at sea. The boats had already been extended outboard on the davits ready for quick lowering. For us, it was a moment of fortunate thought to have escaped lethal attack by such a close margin in what we knew would be the final hours of the European conflict, an involuntary accomplishment to have survived the years of war at sea. Yet there was still the matter of the Japanese war and we had all volunteered for service in the Pacific.

This was not the first time our ship had been threatened by submarines. It had occurred at least twice before, once in the Cabot Strait between Nova Scotia and Newfoundland in company with the Department of Transport's buoy vessel *Lady Laurier,* and again off Shelburne on Nova Scotia's South Shore when we were part of a convoy northbound from Boston to Halifax in April 1945. The small convoy comprised fourteen ships and a minesweeper escort. I was off watch, standing on the stern deck just after dawn when a sub appeared through the mist. On the conning tower a black-clad figure scanned us through binoculars and saluted. The sub fell back slightly into the mist. We were the last ship of four in line B.

The sub commander had apparently followed us close in, then surfaced to pick a plump target. The sound of propellers and stray blips from ship bottoms made it difficult if not impossible for the escort's detection devices to separate and identify the wolf from the sheep. Once on the surface and close in to the convoy, the sub found protection among drifting banks of mist moving over the chill waters of the Gulf of Maine. We were under radio silence and in American coastal waters. When I reported to the bridge, Captain Adamson ordered me to advise our escort minesweeper of the sub sighting by Aldis lamp. Fortunately the mist had cleared somewhat and we made immediate contact before it closed in again. Twenty minutes later we heard a booming sound louder than a depth-charge explosion. Obviously a ship had been torpedoed close by. The next half hour echoed with depth-charge explosions that became progressively more distant and finally ceased. The sub had apparently been hit or had run for cover in deeper water.

A former assistant deputy minister and deputy minister of Veterans Affairs has said that merchant navy fatalities even by enemy action in so-called dangerous waters or in other activities related to training, manning pools or assigned travel as ship crew were "hypothetical deaths." But for an accident of fate, the result perhaps of a nautical mile of searoom and five minutes in time, some of our crew could have been "hypothetically dead" fifty years ago to the day as I write this. To be killed on the last day of the war would have been regrettable, an even greater embarrassment would be inclusion among those gone to their hypothetical reward.

It is obvious that pre-conceived and discriminatory opinions concerning the realities of merchant marine service during wartime have been more than evident during the last five decades. Those attitudes have been encouraged by government, the Royal Canadian Legion, and the National Council of Veterans Associations. It may be informative to examine the actions and attitudes of fifty long years, keeping in mind that while a merchant marine representative was invited to take part in 1994 Remembrance Day ceremonies at the National Cenotaph in Ottawa, it was over the objections of armed forces organizations and the Legion. Representation was only agreed to on condition that a precedent was not being set.

Point Pleasant Park

This photo was taken on December 21, 1943 by the US Coast Guard. The *Point Pleasant Park*, a 10,000 ton dry cargo vessel, was launched in February 1943 at the Davie Shipyards in Lauzon, Quebec. She was sunk by torpedos and gunfire from a German submarine off Capetown, early in 1945.

More than 175 Park-class ships, ranging from 4,700-ton dry cargo vessels to 10,000-ton tankers and general cargo carriers, were launched from Canadian shipyards during World War 2. (Photo: Maritime Museum of the Atlantic, N-18,186)

Prejudice now, prejudice then

Fear of setting precedents is a characteristic common to those elected to public office and particularly their advisers. The same concern has been more than evident for fifty years through the reluctance or perhaps the determination of government, the Royal Canadian Legion and the Royal Canadian Naval Association not to recognize wartime merchant seamen as war veterans.

With the end of hostilities in 1945 those serving in the merchant marine did not have an organization. They were aboard ship or briefly in various ports scattered across the oceans of the world. Consequently, there was little incentive and no practical attempt to establish an association that could represent their interests. An uncertain future was another factor; for those who recalled the Hungry Thirties of recent memory there existed a desire to look for a shore job with some hope of a secure future no matter how humble. Many, if not most, deck and engine-room hands as well as radio operators realized instinctively that Canada's merchant service faced a discouraging future. The Park ships made up the bulk of Canada's wartime merchant fleet. By 1944 Ottawa had already begun to sell them off because they were effectively redundant and could not compete with newer, faster, and better-built vessels on the ways in other countries. Ottawa admitted as much in its sales pitch, letting them go at little more than distress prices.

Opportunities for shore jobs were slight. Most of the time mariners were away from Canada, seldom visiting their home ports and then only for a brief stay. It was a commitment well understood by seamen. Their purpose was to sail aboard their ships whenever and wherever ordered. Yet the reality of the situation did not permit the application of either time or energy to job-hunting. Besides, signing off a ship to gamble on getting work before you were out of money and out on the street proved risky. The mariner's term "on-the-beach" has a precise meaning: ashore and out of work. The almost insurmountable handicap in seeking work ashore hinged on the fact that Armed Forces veterans had preference either by rule or in actual practice. The Reinstatment in Civil Employment Act, which held jobs open for Armed Forces veterans, was rarely applicable to merchant mariners. Very few merchant mariners, perhaps no more than a scattered handful, had come from shore jobs. Most had gone to sea from elementary or high school and a period of unemployment was a common experience.

Adding insult to injury for our group, the government in 1947 amended the Civil Service Act to exclude merchant mariners from qualification as veterans and therefore ineligible for preference. The amendment declared that preference be given to military servicemen. An example of how the original service preference worked was brought home in Ottawa in 1940. I wrote a civil service grade-two clerical exam, and passed 628th out of more than eighteen thousand taking the test. I was told off the record by a government official that my marks were excellent. I was moved down the hiring list, however, by a handful of veterans who saw service in the First World War and also apparently by men invalided out in the first weeks of the 1939 war after only a few months in uniform. I was a young civilian at the time and after the end of hostilities the federal government continued to regard me, and many others, as civilians without veteran status. Fortunately for me, in 1940 the demands for manpower resulted in my being hired almost immediately as a grade-two clerk; it appears most of those higher on the list lacked certain clerical skills such as shorthand, typing, filing, etc.

This discriminatory policy against civilians, whether war veterans or not, continued either in practice or in principle after war's end. In Halifax, a housing development called the Westmount subdivision was built for veterans with families. I was married with an infant son by this time but my application was rejected because I did not qualify as a veteran. With my usual reticence, I wrote to the only Member of Parliament who might be concerned about such discrimination. Clary Gillis was a strong labour advocate, as would be expected from the only CCF MP from the eastern provinces, himself a veteran of trench warfare in the 1914-18 conflict.

In my letter to Mr. Gillis describing my rejected application to the Central Mortgage and Housing Corporation, I suggested that only my natural courtesy prevented me from going to Ottawa with the intention of force-feeding my medals (the 1939-45 Star, the Atlantic Star, and War Medal) to Minister of Transport Lionel Chevrier. Short days later, I received a call from the local CMHC representative, asking me to come out immediately and select my new house. He added that he hoped for his own sake I would do so because he was under strict instructions to approve my application. Our family lived happily in Westmount until our sons were through university and I was transferred by the CBC to Toronto.

I had experienced more than one such rejection in the previous couple of years. Any wonder we felt like the Canadians who had volunteered to serve on the republican side in the Spanish Civil War. Hugh Garner has written of his experiences on returning to Canada after Franco's victory and establishment of a fascist dictatorship. Canadian veterans of the International Brigade found on their return to this country that their passports had been lifted, resulting in their rights as native-born citizens effectively being deliberately ignored. A number of them who later joined the Canadian army in the 1939-45 war gave their lives for a nation that for a time had denied their citizenship. It is interesting that those veterans, battle-tested men, had trouble being accepted by Canadian forces. Suspicion and outright accusations branded them as probable supporters of the international communist conspiracy. Undoubtedly a modest number were communists, but in the 1930s many Canadians fell into that category. Some notably respectable citizens in several provinces had more than a nodding acquaintance with local cells, yet radicalism began to fade or at least move toward the back of troubled minds in direct proportion to job opportunities in a wartime economy.

While many remained carefully in the protective closet of conformity, they could hardly forget the ravages of the Depression on human dignity and pride. It is painful to dwell on the economic adversity that led to the desperation that burned into the hearts and minds of an entire generation. The reflection of faces ravaged by misery and poverty would be etched in the memory of those who had lived through those severe days when people were considered responsible for their own poverty. For many others moving into their late teens and knowing nothing but the mean times of the past decade, war presented the prospect of employment and regular pay either in uniform or in the expanding work force. It is easy to understand why taking the King's shilling amounted to a commitment to risk one's life in the cause of democracy. It was also a welcome opportunity for regular employment. For most young people thoughts of the future were far from their minds. They knew some of their comrades would not survive, but for those who did the future could take care of itself; things could hardly be worse than in the Hungry Thirties. Before hostilities ended, many would learn how close our side had come to defeat or at least a difficult and ever-threatening stalemate. That condition developed when our former ally, the Soviet Union, became a threat to democracy during the Cold War's four decades.

Against the backdrop of a highly uncertain future and the challenges of the immediate postwar years, those who served in Canada's merchant vessels faced double jeopardy. First came the closing of all doors to job opportunities, educational discrimination, and continuation in the gray netherworld of non-recognition particularly evident in non-coastal communities. Whether by accident or design, the work of the merchant service during the Second World War received barely noticeable mention in the censored press that served the Canadian public during the war years. When federal authorities released news that a naval ship had been torpedoed and lives lost, later press coverage listed the names of those killed and missing. Such casualties of war deserved public attention and more. Yet if a tanker was torpedoed and blew up with all her crew killed, news reports were not permitted on grounds of national security. The names were never published later. There can be no argument with this essential safeguard; it was necessary and logical that the enemy should not be informed of cargo losses because of the importance of the supply routes to Europe and Pacific war zones. When merchant seamen lost their lives, the next of kin received only a terse telegram from the federal government.

This curtain of silence surrounding the risk and sacrifice of Canadian merchant seamen continued for many years. Casualty lists for the merchant navy were decades late in gaining their deserved place on monuments to those who died or were missing through enemy action.

Unfairness of opportunity was the rule rather than the exception. The war was over for more than a year before I could find a shore job appropriate to my modest skills and experience. Qualifications really didn't matter much because we non-veterans couldn't get a foot in the door. This applied to the federal civil service and by implication to provincial government employment as well. There existed a calculated and emphatic emphasis on providing jobs for demobilized service persons. Justly so. Our problem centred on our being somewhat akin to non-persons. We knew Canada's merchant marine fleet was slow, tired and lacked government commitment to support and revitalize it now that peace had broken out. Ottawa, or rather more precisely the professionals who advise innocent politicians on various policies, seemed to operate with scant knowledge of the lessons of history. It is a characteristic that extends into our own times.It is one thing to be consigned to limbo, or some facsimile thereof, quite another to be exposed to the lies, damned lies, and statistics of a succession of bureaucrats. One brief example involves the concept of "hypothetical death" as expressed by a federal bureaucrat who appeared to be overly impressed by the Armed Forces and the Royal Canadian Legion in their almost unanimous denigration of those who also served at sea in wartime yet are less than socially acceptable.

In the war years the MN lapel pin served as our only obvious identification as merchant seamen, even though it rarely was recognized as such by the general public except in coastal ports. The British wore the first MN pins seen on our side of the Atlantic, reflecting a decision by authorities to acknowledge that merchant mariners had been participants in the conflict. Ottawa later issued pins with the word Canada above the MN. That was the only symbol of service at sea by the so-called civilians, although they did qualify for war medals. Young merchant seamen going ashore in Halifax, Sydney, Saint John, and St. John's found themselves vastly outnumbered by naval ratings. All too often they were jeered at as being draft dodgers or "zombies," a name applied to those who evaded the possibility of overseas service. That gimmick was a devious device to coat the pill of conscription by calling up people for home service only. At the Halifax army depot, MD6, the home service wicket stood hidden behind a pile of broken chairs. The overseas wicket, however, welcomed all who entered there.

For merchant seamen it was ironic that we were regarded with considerable disdain by young servicemen our own age. Had we taken the King's shilling, would it have been considered taxable income? Being described as a "slacker" after many weeks at sea in the North Atlantic was an unpleasant experience, but it occurred more than once and was the cause of some commendable fistfights. It was arguably difficult for some uniformed plough jockey from Bucktooth, Alberta to understand that some civilians might be seagoing men. This lack of awareness was not helped by the reams of patriotic material in print about service people, much of it narrowly focused toward the navy. To this day, little has been written about the contribution of the army and air force to the security of our Atlantic coastline and beyond.

A letter to a Dartmouth newspaper recalled a further embarrassment suffered by some merchant seamen ashore for a few hours:

Merchant Seamen still treated like dirt

There was a misguided period during World War 2 when a group of women patrolled Halifax streets pinning white feathers on out-of-uniform able bodied young men they considered shirkers.

Their scorn was sometimes horribly misdirected as was the case when they pinned a feather on a young British lad. He was a merchant seaman, in port for a few days of R & R. having just survived his latest of a number of torpedo sinkings. While they performed a vital role in the war effort, merchant seamen warranted and they are not now accorded the heroic status they deserve.

Twelve thousand Canadians served in the merchant marine: 1,200 died, while hundreds more sustained injuries or were captured as POWs.

Their casualty rate was 1 in 10, for the RCAF it was 1 in 16, for the army 1 in 32, and the navy, 1 in 47.

Canada will attempt to make it up to the few remaining seamen of that era during this year's (1994) Remembrance Day Ceremonies across the country. The focus will be on a ceremony in the Peace Tower on Parliament Hill, dedicating a Book of Remembrance to those who died.

But it will be a grudging tribute, today's generation having learned little from the white feather warriors of the 1940s.

And to extend the record, it was indeed a grudging tribute on the part of the Royal Canadian Legion. The Legion opposed the placing of the Merchant Navy Memory Book in the Peace Tower, but had an overnight conversion and agreed to it. They did not want the placement ceremony to be held on Remembrance Day, preferring the Battle of the Atlantic Sunday in May. Pressure was exerted to get the Legion to agree to November 11, and they were also asked to permit merchant seamen representatives to be part of the official party to lay a wreath to the memory of their war dead.

A recent commentary reflects on the obvious intransigence of the Royal Canadian Legion and other veterans groups, including the Royal Canadian Naval Association. Their attitude may be considered an accurate reflection of deliberate discrimination against those who served Canada voluntarily by a succession of governments with landlocked thought processes. During CBC coverage of fiftieth anniversary ceremonies marking the war's end in the UK and the Netherlands, Canadian military historian Jack Granatstein spoke of the magnificent history of Canadian soldiers and the hospitality of the Dutch nation and citizens. Professor Granatstein also said the Canadian government's treatment of the merchant marine was a scandal. He added that they are not recognized as a service or given equality with the military, yet without them we would not be be celebrating the fiftieth anniversary of the end of the Second World War.

A half century earlier folklorist and author Dr. Helen Creighton expressed similar views. As a teenager she had been a participant in volunteer services during the First World War. When the Second World War began, she was at home in Dartmouth taking care of her elderly father and pursuing her research in maritime folklore and traditional music. She is quoted in *An East Coast Port...* as saying:

> "If there is one class of war service which commands the respect of everyone without reservation, it is that of the merchant navy. It is possible that people who live in-

land are not fully aware of the debt we owe them. We who live by the sea look at the merchant ships, the tankers and cargo vessels that come in an out of the harbour. Sometimes they are laden with ice, sometimes they show signs of battle. The life rafts are plainly visible and when the weather is severe and one pictures the plight of men forced to leave their ship and float in one of these for hours or perhaps days, one marvels that men are brave enough to go to sea in such craft.

"There is courage of many kinds. Perhaps at the outset the crews sought adventure and thought it would be exciting to serve in this capacity. That may hold for a time. But many of them have been at sea now for years, and most of them have seen dreadful sights. It must be a horrible experience to see ships sinking all about you, and to know that your turn may well come at any moment.

"The same seamen keep coming back to port. As time goes on, one notices a change in their appearance. Sailors on the whole are a happy lot; much more than in other services. Now however they are showing signs of strain. It isn't that they are any less brave, but one can't go through what they do without feeling the effects eventually. Someone will tell you 'I was worried about Captain so and so; he is on the verge of cracking up.' Sea captains who go to the big wholesale houses for supplies are obviously strained. They tell tales which never reach the papers, and the menace is getting worse all the time. The marvel is that they stay on their jobs. They came to port worried lest the lifeline to Britain be severed altogether because of the submarine's deadly work. After a few weeks in port and kindly treatment, the taut lines relax. They go back to sea and have to face it all over again.

"It seems now that people feel the merchant navy is not getting its full due; that these men should be treated like those in other branches of the service. They are paid much less than men in the U.S. merchant ships but I don't know that this is the main issue. The fault lies in the fact that while soldiers, for instance, are relieved of paying income tax, the men of the merchant navy pay it. Again, it is not the payment of money which irks them but the fact that they are treated like civilians.

"Then again the merchant seaman doesn't wear a uniform. (Merchant officers only wore their uniforms at sea.) All the seaman has to show what work he is engaged in is a pin with the letters MN engraved on it. To those of us who know what it means, it is a badge of the highest honour."

The extent of general ignorance concerning the role of civilian service at sea during the Second World War was particularly apparent and frequently embarrassing to those who eventually learned the extent of their own ignorance. When my ship was tied up in Halifax at one point and I was acting purser for a few days, I was visited by two members of the Royal Canadian Mounted Police looking for information about my brother who was also in the merchant navy. We had lived at the same address during a brief period ashore to upgrade our qualifications. After being rejected by the RCAF for colour blindness early in the war, he had now been called up for military service. The Mounties wanted to know where they could contact him because he had not responded to the call-up notice. When I refused to tell them, they advised that I could be escorted to RCMP headquarters for questioning and there were hints of possible charges. At the time my brother was, I found out later, in the English Channel on a damaged oil tanker being towed into a British port for repairs.

I told the Mounties that I could not leave the ship without the Old Man's permission. At that moment Captain Adamson emerged from the master's day room. "What's this about? Trouble with the police, young man?"

"No, sir. They want to contact my brother and I don't know where he is."

"Well?" The Old Man's cold eyes demanded response from the young constables.

"We are authorized to question this gentleman with reference to his brother."

"Is that so, and pray what authorization do you have to conduct an inquiry aboard a ship registered in the United Kingdom without my permission, which I refuse?"

"We'll report this situation to the navy, sir." One of the young men was not intimidated, which was a mistake when dealing with Captain Bill.

"And you are advised that the navy hasn't one damn thing to do with this ship or my authority. My radio officer has told you he does not know where his brother is and that's that. It is very probable that the brother in question is overseas aboard his ship, and with little wish to respond to a call-up for home service with the rest of you stay-at-homes. Please leave my ship immediately."

The Old Man turned on his heel and brushed through the curtain to his day cabin. The Mounties, a bit pale around the gills, stood up and thanked me then went out on deck and down the gangway. I haven't heard from the RCMP since; it would be interesting to see how they reported the incident.

Our pier was just off Water Street below the Halifax Customs House and parallel to the ferry dock. Our return to home berth was always a welcome break in sea time, offering a few days to enjoy the diverse delights of the old city and to walk on solid ground if only for a short time.

Cable Ship Cyrus Field at Key West, Florida, 1944.

    This Western Union Cableship was built at Ste. Nazaire in 1924 from heavy steel plating from a scraped French battleship. The *Cyrus Field*, 224 feet long with a beam of 34 feet, had cable tanks with a capacity of five hundred miles of standard line. Her home port for many years was Halifax, Nova Scotia, where she shared the Western Union pier with another cable ship, *Lord Kelvin*.

    The ship was named after Cyrus Field, an American who pioneered the development of the first successful trans-Atlantic communications cable. After four attempts, the first trans-Atlantic cable spanning a distance of more than 2,980 kilometres (1,852 miles) across the ocean bottom began operations in 1866. (Photo: Doug Fraser)

Home port, old city

The Market Square stood at the foot of George Street that runs steeply down from the Old Town Clock on the Halifax Citadel to the ferry dock. In addition to commuter traffic carried across the harbour on the car ferries, the vessels were crowded during wartime by civilian workers and service personnel. An airbase at Eastern Passage on the eastern side of the harbour and various army operations, including coastal defence artillery and other security forces, complemented the large naval operation at HM Dockyard. The square was a cobble-stoned triangular space bounded on the south by the red sandstone Customs House looking down on a fountain burbling cheerfully night and day. It provided a refreshing drink for horse or man. The human population though was more attracted to Skip's, an illegal grog shop close by and an honoured relic of rum-running days.

Our ship tied up on the south side of the Cable Wharf, a couple of minutes stroll (or stagger) from Skip's and the ferry landing. With our booze supply under customs seal in port it was occasionally necessary to venture ashore for refreshment. We young people were abstemious to some degree, but the older men from time to time enjoyed a cheering taste of Demerara rum. Water Street served as a link to the great trading days of the past when legal commerce and pseudo-legal privateering enriched the pockets of the Halifax gentry. Their warehouses, now much restored, are the principal feature of waterfront nostalgia.

When war was declared in 1939, Water Street retained much of its characteristic 1800s appearance: solid granite buildings with the traditional thickness and strength, as well as Georgian designs much practised by Britain's military engineers in garrison towns and fortifications in the outposts of Empire. From early dawn to darkness of night, Upper and Lower Water streets echoed with the sounds of steel-tired wagons and slovens drawn by shire horses, the screech of metal on flint and the snap of horsewhips punctuated by the foul language of wagoners. Chandlers' warehouses and cordage sheds stood at waterside, partly on the inshore end of the long wharves that provided convenient docking and storage in the usually well-guarded premises. If rumours are to be credited, a shipwright's auger pierced more than one puncheon of rum and a few gallons of luscious Demerara or Barbados rum were drawn off and the hole sealed with tallow to conceal the wound. Based on sad experience, buyers examined the puncheons carefully before accepting delivery from importers and putting down the cash. Importers and wholesalers were usually located in a compound, reached from Water Street through an archway which was secured by a solid gate and a night watchman accompanied by an unpleasant dog.

Our home base was the Cable Wharf, a broad pier bearing the long gray building that sheltered great chunks of hardware required for undersea cable repairs. Immediately inshore and on solid ground was another structure containing giant storage tanks, in which several hundred miles of line were kept in sea water at constant temperature. A complex series of pulleys and guide rollers permitted the cable to be pulled aboard ship and stored in the vessel's tanks.

When faults such as a cable break or a high-resistance leak developed in an undersea line, we loaded the needed repair stock and sailed for the location of the trouble. Our deck officers were all qualified master mariners; the designated navigation officer bore the responsibility of getting us as close as possible to the fault's location. This was done by precise navigation once the distance from shore at both ends of a cable had been computed. Resistance and capacity values were meticulously charted not only at the time the cable was laid (perhaps fifty years earlier) but on all occasions when repairs had been made on the line and the electrical characteristics corrected for the new material inserted. Once the point of interruption had been determined, the crew lowered a marker buoy and firmly anchored it on the sea bottom. Raising the cable to the surface for repair was not a simple operation. A long tow line drew a grapnel across the cable line until it was hooked; the cable was then hoisted up and buoyed off. That stage of the work completed, the ship's engines at Slow Ahead took us to the general vicinity of the other end of the line still many fathoms deep.

Another grapnel hooked the loose end of the cable, hoisting it to the well-deck. There, the jointer soldered it onto the end of new cable. As the ship proceeded to the buoy supporting the other end, the new joint section was lowered overboard and fresh line paid out of the tank. That one was taken on deck and the second or final splice was completed. The actual joining of the signal line or lines (some cables had three copper wires) was an operation requiring skill and a delicate touch with the soldering iron. The new joint and conductor were insulated with gutta percha tape, wrapped in spunyarn, then re-enclosed in armour wire. The procedure, although simple, was not completed easily. Handling a blow-torch while the well-deck heaved and yawed as wind gusts whistled around the little tent sheltering him attests to the jointer's skill. When completed and wrapped in armour wire and spun-yarn, the splice was returned to the sea. Subsequently, twin conductor lines, lowered and towed along the charted cable line at the necessary depth, picked up the buzz-buzz signal sent from the shore terminus. The signal advised us that the circuit had been restored, and instructed us to proceed to the next repair or to port.

On my initial voyage, just before the war began, I entered Halifax by sea for the first time and our small vessel tied up at the Plant Wharf at the foot of Sackville Street. At that time the property still retained its chandlery buildings that had served as home terminus for the Plant Line ships, passenger and freight vessels on the Boston to Halifax run. The service had been well and profitably established in earlier decades when railway service between Nova Scotia and New England proved long and tedious. The Plant Line had been out of operation for a long time, but the wharf still operated, providing tie-up space to seagoing vessels at reasonable fees. The Plant Wharf was later taken over by an oil company that used the old commercial buildings for office space, including rooms above the archway leading through to the pier.

Fifty-six years after I first stepped ashore there, the old Plant Wharf property would serve as the meeting place for the G-7 Economic Summit held in June 1995. The chandlery shops and wharf-piling has been replaced and the site filled in; it now supports a large green-glass building with its harbour side ressembling the prow of a ship. The G-7 ship of state had, as is usual in such meetings, a number of skippers and little consensus on the proper course to avoid the dangerous shoals of economics and world trade.

In the war days we usually arrived off Thrumcap Shoal at the harbour mouth about midnight. Following identification, the anti-submarine net opened and we were safely inside. With the ship moored alongside and the Finished With Engines sounding on the engine-room telegraph, off-duty married men and those with other commitments of various categories went ashore. Two or three of us living aboard ship dallied briefly in the purser's cabin over a heavy belt of rum meant to ward off the morning chill. We then proceeded down the gangway to renew the experience of walking on solid ground, welcome relief from the constant balancing act needed to remain vertical on a moving deck. We walked through the paved tunnel past the cable storage building to Water Street, proceeding wide-legged and flat-footed after weeks at sea. We continued a couple of blocks south to the Plant Wharf entrance, its protective cannon buried muzzle-up at each side of the archway. Then, we headed up Sackville Street and along Hollis Street toward our destination, an all-night restaurant known with considerable favour as the Sea Grill.

At three on a frosty morn precious few people were about: a passing policeman familiar with the sight of boozy deck-hands at that time of the clock, perhaps an occasional drunk whimpering his request for a few pennies for bread. When asked for booze money, we were inclined to give a few coins in recognition of blatant honesty. After a noble meal of grilled fresh mackerel and a glass of real milk, it was back to the ship for a shower and preparation for ship's business: official entry at the Customs House, the crew list report to immigration, and more. An embarrassing error appeared in one of those reports. In my dual job as radio operator and assistant purser, I worked with Joe Jeffries, the purser and a veteran of the Royal Navy's Air Arm. As a teenager, Joe had been awarded the Distinguished Conduct Medal for heroic action in the North Sea flying boat patrol over hostile waters between Grimsby and the Helgoland Bight.

Our difficulty with immigration occurred by accident. We had been rushing departure preparations because we were seldom, if ever, given more than a few hours notice of sailing time. Ship's papers had to be checked, the crew list verified on the master sheet with necessary changes made to reflect men on leave or invalided ashore and the replacement seamen hired for deck and engine-room crews. How it occurred was never quite clear, but we sailed with one less man aboard than was listed on the immigration form. We discovered the error a day out of port with our next destination Vera Cruz in the Gulf of Mexico. The purser decided to keep the omission secret until we could determine how to solve the problem, if and when we returned to Canada. In the meantime, a man ashore in Halifax was on our crew list and officially out of the country. Safely at sea, we held a bilateral conference on the problem to discuss alternatives: confessing to the Old Man (too dangerous considering his volatile temper), or declaring on return to Halifax that the man had jumped ship in Mexico and was never seen again. If we did that, immigration officials would demand documentation and the seaman's wife would no doubt be notified that her husband had gone ashore in Mexico and had not returned. The lady in question would have been very much puzzled by the news considering that her spouse was at that moment painting the fence in their backyard on Almon Street in Halifax.

Finally, Joe decided that we would bluff it out. We would declare the extra man's presence aboard as listed with immigration, then sign him off in Halifax. The only difference would be that his date of signing-off would be changed and all would be well. But how would we get the Old Man to sign the immigration list if it carried sixty-one names instead of sixty. "To Hell with it, we'll deal with that when the time comes," we said. Time and luck sorted things out. Back in Halifax, the Old Man went on sick leave for a minor operation and the chief officer took command. He was a decent man and trusted implicitly our judgment on what to sign and when. We had to declare that the man in question had changed his mind and wished to re-sign immediately. This was agreed to by the acting-master on grounds of compassion - the seaman's wife had kicked him out of the house owned by her father. It was, and quite probably still is, a criminal offense to make a false declaration to the Department of Customs and Immigration. If there is not yet a statute of limitations on such offences, perhaps it can be arranged. Joe Jeffries is long gone to the Purser's Cabin in the sky, and if questioned I can safely say that it was his decision and I had tried to persuade him otherwise.

Joe was a tall man with pleasant ruddy features and decent in all respects. I retain warm memories of him as a drinking and working companion. Ashore and in civilian clothes he had the dignified posture and general appearance of an accountant, somewhat removed from his years at sea in the 1920s and '30s, much of the time on the UK cargo run to the Levant and assorted Mediterranean ports. He had a fondness for Italian ports such as Genoa, Livorno, and Naples, where he had almost gotten married. But apparently the lady was disinclined to be wed in the Church of England, operated by the British colony in the shadow of Mount Vesuvius. In later life, he married a lady in Newfoundland and they spent their retirement years in the High Cliff district near Southampton on the south coast of England.

On occasion Joe would come ashore in the company of younger officers with the declared intention of ensuring our moral conduct. When fights started, as they sometimes did, we discovered that our purser had a mean left hook and a smashing right hand - both very useful in the gloomy back alleys of the waterfront. He'd been a finalist in the 1918 British Navy light-heavyweight contest. The harbourside district was usually dark and dangerous. With the semi-blackout in effect, officials ordered that low-intensity lights and shades be used in cities and towns on the Atlantic coast to prevent reflected glare from the bottom of low-level clouds. The glare would be a convenient focal point for the interest of enemy aircraft or submarines.

German submarines cruised off our coast very early on in the war, contrary to the stupidly sincere conviction of senior Ottawa bureaucrats. The subs could and did sink many merchant ships off our coasts with many "hypothetical deaths." The thickness of federal skulls was never more evident than when Ottawa bureaucrats suggested that bonfires be lit in major cities from coast to coast in support of a national war bond drive. Press editorials and, in less polite terms, the Nova Scotia government advised that Halifax was under semi-blackout, and for good reason: the dogs of war were dangerously close to the homeland.

On one occasion, we were returning to port when we were advised by radio to stop the ship and anchor immediately. A minelayer submarine had dropped sixty magnetic mines and they were moored in the shipping channel. We had to heave-to with several other ships until the minesweepers cleared the path for us. We used to call the magnetic mine danger German roulette. The mines had a device that was clicked over by the magnetic field of a steel ship passing over it. It might blow up when the first or second or even third ship passed, depending on the sequence of clicks required by the mine's control mechanism.

German aircraft did not have the reserve fuel to attack the northeast coast of North America. That threat was discounted until General Doolittle of the United States Air Force led a bombing attack on Tokyo. His planes continued on, landing in China. From then on, the possibility of a suicide attack on a major convoy port and ammunition facility was not out of the question. A relatively small aircraft might be launched from a shrouded catapult on a merchant vessel under a neutral flag and with a certified cargo in case the vessel was stopped and searched off shore. The flag would be changed and at worst the ship could be scuttled and the crew captured. After the pilot dropped the bomb he would parachute into the spruce where he would, if lucky, be found by search dogs before local citizens caught him and broke both his knees in revenge. Unless it hit the magazine at Burnside on Bedford Basin, the relatively modest bomb explosion would be largely symbolic in damage potential, but still capable of killing people and causing fire damage.

Citizens of the Halifax–Dartmouth–Bedford area understandably were nervous about explosives stored ashore or aboard ship in the vicinity. In 1917 the Norwegian registered *SS Imo*, under charter for Belgian war relief, collided in the harbour Narrows with the French munitions ship *Mont Blanc*. The collision occurred half a mile from where this is being written. The *Mont Blanc* caught fire; her holds carried TNT and a deck cargo that included additional explosives. The subsequent explosion killed more than 1,500 men, women, and children with hundreds more maimed and injured. My father was 1,200 feet underground in the Allan Shaft coal mine, a hundred miles away in Stellarton. He told me the power of the biggest man-made explosion sent out a shock wave that shattered a heavy slate switching panel. His first thought focused on a possible gas explosion in the mine. It would be another quarter century before the Halifax Explosion would be exceeded by the nuclear bomb dropped on Hiroshima. The population of Halifax understood that they were continually on war alert. The fear of another ammunition explosion remained strong in the minds of those who had experienced the 1917 disaster.

As the principal port of departure for the thousands of cargo vessels and scores of troopships crossing the turbulent North Atlantic to the United Kingdom, the great harbour and the Bedford Basin anchorage were potential targets for sabotage. The population received constant reminders that security was a fragile condition and that a casual word might find its way into enemy ears. Whether German spies actually operated in the area has never been revealed in postwar histories. In retrospect, it is logical that the enemy would collect and forward information on convoy sailings to Berlin. As always, accidents were freely ascribed to saboteurs. This was true in 1945 when a fire and explosion at the ammunition depot on the east side of Bedford Basin caused the evacuation of the northern section of the Halifax peninsula. Thousands of people spent the night hours huddled under blankets on the Halifax Common, where they were shaken by a second early morning explosion of stored depth charges.

The tense atmosphere of war became part of every day life in a city in which uniforms of all Allied nations were seen on the streets, including New Zealand and Australian airmen proceeding to Britain after the long Pacific crossing and the train journey from Vancouver. Barrington Street in the evening hours represented a moving panorama of uniformed people, standing in theatre line-ups or enjoying a relaxed visit in a community they knew was the last stop before entering a war zone immediately beyond the gate vessels. Although no one thought much about it at the time, there existed a common understanding that we were caught up in the progress of momentous times. The most adventurous people with little interest in history seemed to understand that their safety and, in many cases, their lives would be the price of a front-row window on war. It seemed that everyone generally accepted the obligation to make any sacrifice for the cause of freedom. This may have been partly due to the authoritarian menace of the Axis powers. Yet, there was something more: a system of education in the Empire, in pre-Commonwealth times, that gave equal place to obligation and basic learning.

My brother remembers that when he was on an American passenger ship in the Black Sea, the ship's navigator advised that their course lay between the Clashing Rocks. It recalled memories of the grade-five reader and the story of Jason and the Argonauts hastily pulling the *Argo* between the giant rocks which opened briefly to let a dove fly through. Legends have the quality of lasting longer than facts or the historical version of great events. To a person who grew up hearing first-hand the stories of war from men returned from the trenches of Flanders, the few who agreed to talk about their experiences, it was an introduction to history. Yet the stirring tales were of a time as remote to a lad as the Battle of Marathon. Then, on September 3, 1939, what had been adventure stories for young minds became a chilling yet enticing prospect. Even as memories fade of a half century past, it may be wondered how many individuals, rejected as physically or genetically unfit for service in the Armed Forces, voluntarily served in the merchant marine. They would deserve the title of conscientious non-objectors.

The wreckage of the Imo — December 1917, Halifax harbour.

The *Imo*, a Norwegian ship chartered to the Belgian Relief Committee, collided with the French ammunitions ship, *Mont Blanc* in Halifax harbour, December 6, 1917. The fire on the French ship spread to its deckload cargo of explosives. The crew of the *Imo* took to the lifeboats and reached the Dartmouth shore in time to gain a few hundred yards up the slope before the *Mont Blanc* blew up, taking much of the north ends of Halifax and Dartmouth with her.

The *Imo's* deckhouse damage and twisted hull plates were quickly repaired and she was immediately renamed the *SS Gouvernoren*. Built in Belfast in 1889 by Harland and Wolff as the *SS Runic*, she served the White Star Line as a livestock carrier on the North Atlantic run. In 1912, she was sold to Norwegian interests, renamed, and sailed in the whaling waters of the North Pacific. After the Halifax Explosion she was used as a whale factory ship. In 1920 she was wrecked on a reef near Port Stanley in the Falkland Islands. (Photo: Maritime Museum of the Atlantic #5295)

SS Kronprinsessen — Halifax, July 1942

The *Empire Latimer*, with a gross tonnage of 7,244, was built at Sunderland, UK, in 1941. The Norwegian government bought her in 1942 and renamed her *Kronprinsessen*.

While on a New York–Halifax–London convoy, she was hit by a torpedo from a German submarine. Determined to save his cargo of steel, flour and cotton, the captain called for tugs from Halifax and Boston. She limped to the Pubnico area of Nova Scotia. Despite the fact food was rationed during the war, the captain and crew were ordered to dump the flour bales overboard. The RCMP received orders to bombard local residents with water cannon to stop fishermen from retrieving the flour. Some braved the spray, while others waited for the bales to float their way. Many families in the area had enough salvaged flour for a year or two. Evelyn Richardson, one of the keepers of the Bon Portage lighthouse on Nova Scotia's south shore, told the sad tale in her book *B was for Butter and Enemy Craft*. (Photo: Maritime Museum of the Atlantic, Halifax, NS)

Ships, convoys, and casualties

Convoy outward bound; the mist moves in from the sea with the smell of salt and far-off places as the giant fleet lies ready in Bedford Basin. The gray shapes are hulls down to the Plimsoll line marked WNA (Winter North Atlantic), the recommended safe burden for the western ocean. Tankers lie deep with petroleum and more volatile fuels. Cargo ship holds are full and deck cargoes include tanks and aircraft shrouded in protective cocoons that give gross distortion to their silhouettes. The twin-tailed fighter planes, with their wheels cradled in steel frames welded to the deck bolts, look like giant insects with gently curving skin glistening in the moist air of early morning. The brooding hulks of tanks are softened by their anti-corrosion garment, surreal as though the tools of battle are exhibits in some museum of the future, reminders of past conflicts in a time when wars would be no more than faded recollections in dusty volumes of history. Seen at close range, the assemblage brought memories of a boy's reading of great land campaigns when hostile armies moved over the sandy plains of northern Europe and caravans of conquest trailed across the eastern steppes. In the conflict of nations, men fought bravely, but supplies could and did sway the balance between victory and defeat.

Before the dawn, ships weigh anchor in Bedford Basin and begin to slip through the Narrows, past corvettes secured alongside and cranes towering over the storage sheds and repair shops of His Majesty's Dockyard. To starboard, the granite buildings of ship chandlers, banks, and the business of government slip by under the looming presence of the Citadel. Each in succession passes the downtown of old Halifax, a shipping port since 1749, when it began civic existence as a safe harbour for the British muscle meant to balance the power of France at Louisbourg and Quebec. George's Island to port and the long seawall to starboard, the ships move through the outer harbour to Mauger's Point lighthouse where gate vessels open anti-submarine nets. It would take many hours for the sixty-four ships to proceed from the Basin to Sambro Lightship, ten miles out, and begin convoy formation. All vessels anchored in the Basin moored at specific points. The departure schedule called for sequential sailing to ensure vessels remained in correct numerical order through the narrow opening between the Dartmouth shore and the steep slope of Fort Needham on the western side of Chebucto Bay, the Micmac name for the giant harbour.

Convoy planning is a complicated and precise art. The hundreds of convoys dispatched from Halifax resulted in teams gaining wide experience in what was, with rare exception, a highly efficient operation, involving the movement of a million tons of deadweight steel and lading through the tight channel toward open water. The UK Ministry of War Transport, in close cooperation with Canadian authorities and the naval command, controlled convoy movements. The system seemed to work rather well, mainly because principals in the operation toiled in close harness and knew their respective trades. The ministry employed various services, directed from its offices in a harbourside shipping agency close to the naval command.

Roy Gilkie was the boss of three harbour craft responsible for messages and general surface communication with ships anchored in the Basin, moored on the Dartmouth side, and at the line of wharves along the waterfront streets of Halifax. Toward the harbour mouth, the seawall occupied a third of a mile of concrete pier, long enough to moor the largest ships and with remaining room for two smaller ones. At that seawall, the *Queen Mary* and *Queen Elizabeth* embarked a full division of troops, ten thousand men, and carried them to the shores of England and the training fields of Salisbury Plain. The port was overcrowded during the wartime years. Harbour pilots and service staff with their relatively tiny boats faced continuing challenges from the weather, collision with vastly larger craft, and the ever-present risk of falling from a jacob's ladder, its treads shiny with ice. Roy Gilkie arrived at the ministry office in mid-afternoon, when the sixty-four master mariners met with the convoy commodore. The commodore, a retired big-ship Cunarder, had wide experience in the western ocean aboard the red-stack ships, their funnels the distinctive colour that identified descendants of the early fleet of Sir Sam Cunard, who made his mark and his first real money as a shipowner based in Halifax. As the meeting concluded and the square-jawed and square-shouldered skippers trooped down the creaky varnished stairs, Roy received his instructions for the following day. The sailing information, convoy position, sequence of departure, convoy formation and ships positions in it, general communications instructions, emergency routing and rendezvous orders had all been consigned to the hands of the captains. If late changes were required, Roy would deliver them. The ships would proceed in sequence out of the harbour to form up in convoy off Sambro. The course would be set eastward, and the flotilla would spread over many miles of ocean. Station-keeping would be a constant and demanding test for captain, deck officers, and lookouts, particularly when weather worsened, as it did rather often between Cape Race and the United Kingdom.

Roy's boat was thirty-five feet long and broad of beam, ten feet of bottom that gave her stability. Her power was considerably greater than the ordinary duty boat serving harbour needs. Roy had spent most of his life since a boy in boats and in constant study of the elements and their possible and probable dangers. His task, difficult in good weather and of heavy stress when the weather was bad, involved delivering essential information to help speed the convoy on its way. Now eighty-five, his physical stamina must have been remarkable to climb up a rope ladder then down sixty or more times in eight hours, sometimes less, sometimes longer. Ships anchored close together and the running time from one delivery to the next often five minutes or less. The hard sweat of constant vigilance as he climbed up the ladder and down hardened an already strong physique.

His grandfather and father were lighthouse keepers on Sambro Island, on the western side of the Halifax harbour approaches. As a boy he learned the practical skills of boat handling, managing the light and the fog-gun. He absorbed the mystery of the sea at close range as vessels of all sizes and flags passed within close range of his German-made binoculars. His knowledge of tides, winds and the treacherous currents of coastal waters developed early. By his teens he knew how to handle small craft and had some knowledge of engine repair and carpentry skills. He and his father built boats on the island and when the family moved to Melville Cove on Halifax's Northwest Arm in 1929, they established the Gilkie boatyard. In 1939 Roy Gilkie was foreman in his father's boatyard. When war broke out, Charles Johnson, a young man previously employed at the yard, received a call-up for military service. He was then working for the UK Ministry of War Transport in its Halifax operation and there was a vacancy.

The ministry contacted Roy, asking if he knew a suitable replacement. He didn't at the moment but volunteered to fill in for a couple of weeks while they looked for a new employee. Whether they looked hard or not, when the two weeks ended Roy was told he could not leave because he was working in an essential job. He had applied for enlistment in the RCAF Marine Section and passed medical tests. When he reported for duty, he was advised that instructions were received that Gilkie, Roy, could not be accepted: he was in essential war work. He went back to the ministry and threatened to quit, but was told if he did he would be declared a deserter from essential war work; he would be black-listed and would never again work in Canada. That was when Roy demanded, and got, better pay for himself and his crew. He remained on the job until 1945, almost six years of long days as chief boatman for the harbour craft that served the ministry's communications needs in port operations, including the essential task of assembling and dispatching convoys out of Halifax. The ministry advised that he would be making a major contribution to the monumental task of getting many thousands of troops and millions of tons of supplies overseas: "The United Kingdom and Allied forces depend on the convoys you help to send." It was Roy's call to arms and he had been told by the air force that he could contribute much more with the ministry than he would as a boatman with the RCAF Marine Section.

On the second floor of the Furness-Withy office on upper Water Street, a typical ship chandlery and marine agency, Roy began at eight o'clock in the morning with the daily review of plans and the state of convoy preparations. Around the polished table the movement of millions of tons of supplies and armament each month was carefully planned and expedited. Ministry people pulled all the details together, civil, military, fueling needs, and food and water supplies.

In Roy's words:

"Our first task each day was to transfer ship's officers and Ministry of War Transport officials up to the Basin to ships that would be sailing in convoys ranging in size from thirty vessels to as high as eighty.

"We had many and frequent jobs to carry out: delivery of information packages and requirements of various kinds, so many extra tasks came up when sailing time neared. The ministry's responsibility covered a broad range of marine requirements.

"Our boat was sturdy and seaworthy but not very big, only thirty-five feet long. We worked in all weather, most of it bad, especially in the winter months. No matter the conditions or time of night, when we were called, we were ready.

"As head boatman I had to meet every big ship at the harbour gates and accompany them in to the seawall. At three o'clock one winter morning with snow falling and the dampness cutting to the bone, we welcomed the *Queen Mary* and kept abeam of her to port as she moved slowly toward the pier. It was my duty, and mine alone, to pick up the snubbing line dropped from her stern and get it over to the pier, where shore hands used it to pull in the heavy hawser and loop it around the bollard. Then the ship's winch tightened the hawser and pulled her stern in slowly to the concrete pier. Seven tugs were outside, pushing her side on toward the berth.

"The giant ship's stern line was solidly snubbed, but on this occasion we had a problem. We were supposed to keep our boat outside the line so we would be clear when it was tightened. But signals were mixed perhaps and we were caught inside with nowhere to go but for'ard with the hope we could move the thousand feet fast enough to escape being crushed like a peanut shell.

"We were caught in the narrowing alley between 85,000 tons of steel ship and the concrete seawall.

"There was no chance of escape. We couldn't climb the concrete wall and the giant hull was seventy feet high. Our only chance, and it would be close, very close, would be to power up ... I hollered to my deckhand 'Full Ahead, quick!' and the engine roared up to speed.

"The propeller caught and we jumped ahead but it seemed so slow, the ever-narrowing lane closing in on both sides like a very high and very narrow mountain pass.

"We had three six-inch fenders on either side of the boat and as we moved ahead the ship kept closing in. We had made about three hundred feet, when three fenders on the ship side rolled up on deck as the hull plates scraped our starboard gunwale. We picked up speed and after making another four hundred feet the fenders on the inward wide rolled up on the deck and we were now down to inches. The stern wave of our propeller turning at full speed in the narrow space gave us a bit of extra shove and we cleared with maybe a couple of inches to spare.

"It was the closest I ever came to getting killed, not just killed, squashed flat. But I was too busy to think about it at the time. We knew there was always danger in the harbour, so much traffic, bad weather, and on the water accidents can happen any time no matter how careful you are."

After more than fifty years his memory of the big squeeze remains sharp.

Orders to sail 5:00 am, June 25, 1943. Anchors aweigh. The first ship in the order of departure moves Slow Ahead toward the Narrows; she will be followed at intervals of five to eight minutes by succeeding vessels. The long journey to an undisclosed destination is well under way in the lightening hours, the sun hanging above the horizon beyond the Dartmouth hills. Frame houses and hospital buildings at Woodside reflect on the harbour surface with only a fading ripple from the Dartmouth–Halifax ferry. The shipyard hammers are silent in the quiet of night, but maintenance gangs are already at work at the graving dock as the ships move down channel to the sea. The gate vessels had been signalled to open the steel-cabled anti-submarine barrier stretching out from Mauger's Light toward Portuguese Cove. In a few hours, sixty-four ships and a million tons of war cargo would be forming into convoy position off Sambro Light, setting course eastward toward the battlefields of Europe.

The naval escort ships were already at sea, providing a tightly screened patrol fore and aft and on both flanks of the armada. It was a watch that would continue for the long days of pushing through the northern sea to Britain's western approaches. Aboard the commodore ship, the senior officer checked signal procedures that he had already reviewed several times and would read again. For smaller convoys, such as those on the St. John's–Halifax–Saint John–Boston–New York run, the commodore could be an aging merchant captain, creaky but called out of retirement. On the cross-ocean convoys, the commodore would be a retired naval reserve commander or captain with decades of blue-water experience. The responsibilities required constant vigilance by the commodore and his staff. With absolute radio silence, ships in convoy were advised by lamp signals if they strayed from their station in the floating grid of steel ships. It wasn't easy communicating by blinking lights with masters and deck officers from a half dozen nations, some of them slow in English and others with less fluency, not to mention the many officers with little practice in reading visual signals. It required patience and more patience. The escorts were busy enough with their constant undersea sonar sweeps for submarines, but they could and did order stray cargo ships back into line when visibility from the commodore ship was poor.

The eastward course from Nova Scotia was variable, depending on the intelligence information which estimated, perhaps guessed at, the probable or possible position of submarine wolf packs. They could be operating anywhere in the wide expanse of ocean, but they much preferred waters south of Iceland beyond the range of shore-based aircraft. Mid-ocean was the danger point, and in the Battle of the Atlantic one in four merchant mariners leaving Halifax was lost, their ships torpedoed. Even so, many more submarines prowled in other parts of the Atlantic from the Flemish Cap east of Newfoundland, along the coastal areas of the Atlantic provinces and New England, and into the Caribbean. Loaded tankers on the long haul from Aruba and other oil ports north to New

York, Boston, or Halifax were favoured targets. Some served American and Canadian energy pools, but most were destined for United Kingdom ports.

The convoy out of Halifax on June 25, 1943, included twelve tankers, most carrying diesel fuel. One or two — such information was not circulated — were loaded with high octane and highly volatile aircraft fuel. If torpedoed, the explosion would light the sky and spread small pieces of steel and bodies over the seascape. Some seconds later, the slamming sound of the explosion would blast the eardrums of sailors and vibrate the hull plates of ships miles distant. Many masters and crew said later they were under considerable tension while in port, perhaps thinking of the ordeal ahead. But once under way and in convoy, except in times of emergency, the routine of shipboard life had a soothing effect. We were frightened, but serving watches, sleeping in heavy weather with the bunk board propped up by a book, and, if in a known danger area, keeping warm in a life-jacket, snug as a teddy bear.

Life-jackets came equipped with a battery-powered red signal light to be used by a mariner floating in the water to alert rescue ships which accompanied the convoys in the later years of the war. On one occasion, I was asleep with the jacket on in a smaller coastal convoy off the Cabot Strait. Submarines were about. I had been dreaming about proceeding through a narrow channel and when I awoke, seeing what I thought was the starboard running light of another ship. In my sleep, I had turned on my rescue light.

If required to abandon ship, we had rubberized survival suits, pants and a jacket. Part of the pants assembly included serrated rubber soles to secure a better grip on slippery decks. The yellow suits were all of one size, very large. Black ribbon ties secured the waistline and rubberized cape, which was part of the installation. Other tapes allowed you to fold up and tighten the pants around the knees. If you didn't get the air out of the lower legs first, however, you could fall overboard and float around, looking like the Michelin Man with feet in the air, the rest of you under water. It was difficult to get upright again, even though we'd practised it a bit. Heat inside the rubberized envelope could give an extra hour or so of life, instead of the few minutes afforded with exposure to the cold northern sea.

Pre-sailing preparations by the chief officer included inspection of safety equipment. In addition to life-jackets and survivor's suits, crews on British ships were issued with gas-masks and khaki army helmets, relics of the First World War. The ship's radio room came equipped with a sturdy canvas bag, a foot in diameter and three feet high with the base weighted with lead for fast sinking in case the code books it held were thrown overboard. The Admiralty required that procedure in the event the ship was torpedoed, in a collision, or grounded. Rumours circulated about the total loss of a ship when she piled ashore on a rocky coast of the Atlantic provinces, where an unfriendly shore is the rule rather than the exception. During the war, such events were not publicized and no one knew, other than the authorities, if the crew had gotten safely ashore or were smashed to bits in the attempt.

After the seas died down a couple of days later, a shore party was able to get aboard what remained of the doomed ship. There was no sign of life but the radio room door was open and the weighted bag lay open on the floor, the code books on the desk. Apparently the radio man had it ready for jettisoning but may have looked out on the boat deck for a moment and been swept off by a heavy wave just as the ship smashed down and broke her back on the rubble of broken rock below the cliff. There was hell to pay, including dire warnings to ship masters and their radio officers that such defiance from or avoidance of orders would not be tolerated. Naval and civil authorities in Halifax, Ottawa, and especially London were furious, facing the immediate need to issue new sets of code books and ensure that old ones had been destroyed, with witnesses. It was an expensive operation and had to be done quickly. Ominous threats of the dungeon or masthead hangings awaited further infractions. It was assumed the radio officer had been drowned, if he was lucky.

The general view pervaded that officials over-reacted to the affront. It was probably about time the code books were changed anyway. Admiral Doenitz probably had them in his command office in Kiel or Wilhelmshaven or wherever he flew his flag. Teutonic efficiency would have long since had them copied and issued with the final rations as U-boats slipped out of their concrete nests and headed nor'west toward Stavanger and the Norwegian Sea and the open Atlantic. Before sailing, convoy ships were battened down and ready for sea. Lifeboats had been swung out on their davits, braced on padded spars, and securely lashed to the inward stanchions. The boats swung out over the water and ropes hung free from the head rope between the davits. In an emergency, men could slide down in seconds and take the oars to fend off the ship before placing them in the oarlocks and pulling away to safety.

At eight bells on the afternoon of June 26, 1943, into the first dog watch, the convoy out of Halifax is proceeding due south of Sydney, and north of the twenty-mile crescent of Sable Island's sands. Course is set over the Grand Banks, south of Cape Race on the southeastern tip of Newfoundland. Fog may be expected. Thick sea mists are not unusual on the banks and each ship is ready with its fog buoy. The leading edge slants upward and in the middle a scoop is installed to throw up a spray of water and greatly increase the ship's visibility through the mist. The plume of water informs the lookout and bridge officers aboard the ship following astern that they are in position just aft of number C4, the fourth ship in column three of the convoy. If the fog is too thick to follow the one ahead, captains will order ships to drop to half or perhaps quarter speed, while masters, mates, and lookouts quickly repent of their sins and reach for a prayer book. After hours, and sometimes days, of eye strain and slow progress, the mists clear and visibility is good which is an indication of heavy weather approaching. The prospect of imminent submarine attack gets closer every hour.

Past the Flemish Cap, a steep rise in the ocean floor east of Newfoundland, and approaching the cockpit of danger south of Iceland, the cruel boom boom of depth charges rattles the hull plates. A mushrooming explosion on the convoy's starboard quarter obliterates a tanker and her crew. Escort ships close in on the area, while others maintain careful watch where they expect more subs of the wolf pack wait to take advantage of a diversion. First one pattern of depth charges, then another, at various distances and directions from the convoy line. Now, flags go up on the commodore ship and the vessels are ordered to disperse rather than remain as sitting ducks. Engineers pile on a knot or two but the heavily laden ships can't move much faster. The ships scatter into the lowering mist and to safety, perhaps. Then after twenty-four hours of following the evasive patterns intended to result in the convoy reforming, half the number of the original group join up, escorted by a destroyer and two corvettes. Some stragglers would be picked up by other escorts and might be tacked on to convoys going into Reykjavik to join UK-bound groups. The convoy out of Halifax reformed, but with twelve fewer ships. In ensuing days, only the Admiralty would know the final toll or the number of stragglers located.

On the eight hundred miles into UK waters and under the umbrella of coastal aircraft squadrons patrolling the western approaches, two single-sub attackers were driven off. After one merchant ship received severe damage but remained afloat, a spare escort shepherded her in at slow speed. The convoy proceeded past the Isle of Lewis off northwest Scotland and into Loch Ewe, seventeen days after leaving Halifax. Some ships would join the next convoy bound for Murmansk, others would be diverted south to discharge cargo at the Clyde or Liverpool and reload for the next departure westward to North America.

After weeks at sea, entering the securely defended anchorage of Loch Ewe required concentration; it had to be done quickly and efficiently. Recalls Captain Ken Moore of Halifax, then a boy in his teens:

> "I was on the bridge with the Aldis lamp, responding to the identification challenge from the signal station on the headland at the entrance to Loch Ewe. I was a very young apprentice (cadet in deck-officer training) and since most of the officers were middle-aged men and their merchant service in peacetime gave them little practice in lamp signalling, I was ordered to perform.
>
> "Ships entering the loch were ordered to signal the name of their ship, call letters, name of captain, final destination, and cargo. There was a code word for final destination, in case a spy's eye ashore would be watching.
>
> "I began our signal some distance off the entrance and had to work reasonably fast because all information had to be received by the shore authorities before the vessel entered. The shore station signallers were WRNS, members of the Women's Royal Naval Service, and they were good, very good. They could read code as fast as human hands could transmit the letters, perhaps faster. Efficient, precise, and obviously well trained. Then too, the best graduates of the signal schools would be assigned to the most sensitive posts.
>
> "When we left Loch Ewe and formed up in convoy, the thoughts of a teenaged apprentice were on the massive steel ship heading into submarine territory under the guns of the Luftwaffe, and the vicious cold and savage weather of the northern lati-

tudes. Memories are deep and still sharp in mind. To qualify as a master mariner in later years was gratifying but faded in comparison with the ultimate fact of survival."

At sea and up through the North Minch and on course toward the everlasting ice of the Arctic Circle and beyond; ahead, 1,500 nautical miles through the gauntlet of frozen hell, under threat from massed attack by submarines and the fury of German bombers, within two hours flight from their principal nests at Bandfjoss and Banak on Norway's northeast coast.

The Murmansk run was the most dangerous convoy in the history of sea warfare with the possible exception of the brief flurry of Japan's kamikaze or suicide attacks on US naval forces in the closing weeks of the Pacific war. British naval forces were assigned to the Murmansk/Archangel convoys in strength: battleships, heavy and light cruisers, destroyers, and frigates as well as support vessels. The heavy metal aboard battleships and cruisers was necessary insurance if the pocket battleships *Scharnhorst* and *Gniesenau* ventured forth from their secluded anchorage in the fjords of southern Norway. If those venomous ships got through Britain's naval screen across the North Sea from Bergen to the Orkneys, slow-moving convoys would be sitting ducks. Eight days of constant alert, waves that seemed as high as the Blackpool Tower and the breath-stopping chill of winds from the frontyard of the north pole; torpedoings, depth-charge explosions past counting and the daily demonstration of anti-aircraft ordnance from the cruisers and destroyers. Approaching the North Cape, Russian cruisers and destroyers closer to the cruiser category joined with the Allied naval units in putting up a screen of steel projectiles that almost covered the gray skies. The heat of attack increased as the convoy changed course eastward past Bear Island and into the Barents Sea where Murmansk and Archangel sheltered south of the Kola Peninsula.

The tools of war delivered to our Russian allies, the ships would retrace their course, past the pack ice and through the guns, gales, and air attacks to the far-away shelter of Loch Ewe. Some would return to Halifax for another run. As his ship moved slowly toward the harbour entrance, one young officer scanned the cluttered port and snow-covered treeless hills surrounding Murmansk. The cold wind whipped through the bridge window and frosted his eyebrows: "It was a place you were glad to leave, even knowing that the return voyage would be as rough and tough as the long sea miles from Scotland north. What choice was there to make your own decisions about your own safety and security, when we were all working for George, (6th) Liege Lord of All the Empire. We only hoped to hell the danger and sacrifice was in a good cause. The immediate challenge was to survive long enough for a look at the postwar world — win, lose, or draw."

From June 21, 1941, to May 8, 1945, one hundred and four Allied merchant ships were lost on the Murmansk/Archangel run, perhaps two million tons of cargo and twelve hundred lives. The British Navy lost two cruisers, seven destroyers, two sloops, one frigate, three corvettes and four mine-sweepers. Casualty figures were proportionally high.

SS Martin Van Buren
The *Martin Van Buren*, an American Liberty ship of 7,176 gross tonnage, was built at Bethlehem Fairfield Shipyard in 1943 for the US War Shipping Administration. This design was susceptible to breaking apart just forward of the main deckhouse. Later models had a band of triple-riveted steel for greater strength and hull stability. The remains of the *Martin Van Buren* and another Liberty ship were towed into Halifax harbour and beached on McNab's Island. (Photo: Maritime Museum of the Atlantic, W. Young Collection #N-23065)

Recognition: vanishing dream

The intransigence of a generation of politicians and senior bureaucrats is more than history, it reflects a mind-set still evident in spite of lip-service to the principle of merchant navy recognition.

In recent years, legislation drawn with the declared purpose of correcting this half century of neglect has only added to the confusion. Whether deliberate or not, the interpretation of recognition and benefits proclaimed by the Secretary of State for Veterans Affairs is more than inconsistent with the actual legislation. On March 10, 1995, Secretary of State Lawrence MacAulay said in a letter to Francis LeBlanc, MP that all current benefits administered by Veterans Affairs Canada (VAC), such as disability pensions, allowances, and health care, are now available to qualified individuals. That statement is based on provisions of Bill C-84, the Merchant Navy Veterans and Civilian War-Related Benefits Act as enacted in July 1992.

Many people with sympathy for merchant navy veterans could and did gain the impression that past wrongs had been corrected. Understandably so, considering the carefully crafted public relations effort of VAC's professional communicators. "Available to qualified individuals" is the soggy apple in this barrel of platitudes. Interpretation of "qualified individuals" is the nettle and the convenient means of allowing federal authorities to define conditions in favour of their own position. It may be noted that VAC opposed awarding the Canadian Voluntary Service Medal to wartime merchant mariners until three-quarters of them were dead of natural causes, principally old age. The reality is that merchant marine veterans are still attempting to collect benefits supposedly provided for under the Act; exemptions listed in the Act continue the decades-long discrimination. The very dangerous waters along the eastern seaboard of the United States and Canada, including the Gulf of Saint Lawrence, are excluded from consideration in disability claims or death benefits to surviving widows. Scores of ships were sunk within five to a hundred miles out in coastal waters, but again the dead and injured are enshrined in bureaucratic history as "hypothetical" victims.

Since the new program was announced, the federal government has set aside more than $17 million per year for merchant navy benefits. In the first year only $1 million was paid out; $3 million in the second. At that pace, a substantial balance will exist when the last merchant navy veteran is dead. Our federal masters and their willing henchpersons are adept at saving money by deliberately delaying the process established to authenticate claims. Their efforts appear slow and inefficient. An air of suspicion suggests we are seen as people looking for handouts, a view shared by veterans organizations. A long-time member of the Royal Canadian Legion told me at a senior citizens meeting in Halifax: "You fellows haven't any records." It may be admitted that access to war records is a problem, but that is mainly due to their dispersal among departments and archival sources in Ottawa; they await cataloguing.

Veterans Affairs Canada, reflecting government policy over the years, has had little if any interest in people who had gone to sea during the war years but were not officially considered or accepted as part of Canada's contribution to the western alliance. In VAC's presentation to the House of Commons committee on June 8, 1993, the deputy minister stated a significant and troubling aspect of federal policy. He said no equity issue required rectifying, although he did indicate that programs extended to veterans of military service and merchant seamen differed. An intriguing point indeed for those who appreciate the nuances of paradox sheathed in vague generalities. Yet in letters on April 8 and April 30, 1993, the then Minister of National Defence Kim Campbell admitted there was inequality.

In response to a question, VAC claimed that most merchant seamen were not in manning pools, the depot system organized to provide bed and board to seamen waiting to join merchant ships and survivors of torpedoed ships waiting for the next berth. Arthur Randles, Director of Merchant Seamen, said in October 1944 that most merchant seamen were in manning pools. Two years earlier, he had advised that the system was working well and no hiatus existed between a seaman paying off from the pool and reporting to a ship. There is a certain logic to this: if a seaman was assigned to a ship and did not report to the shipping office, he was on the beach with no pay, no bed, and little money to buy food.

There is another aspect of government policy that warrants detailed examination: the status of Newfoundland merchant marine veterans subsequent to the Crown colony joining Canada in 1949. Once Newfoundland became part of Canada, its military veterans received the same benefits as Canadian service people. Under the Confederation Agreement, Newfoundland seamen were recognized as members of the Allied merchant service. Although not Canadian citizens prior to 1949, they became eligible for benefits and services as are Newfoundland's military veterans. It may be observed that Allied military veterans living in Canada for ten years can receive benefits, while Allied merchant marine veterans are ineligible.

VAC's refusal to accept claims that the term "dangerous waters" should be an acceptable definition in place of "high seas" is seen as reflecting the opposition of military veterans' organizations.

Yet there is no such differentiation in the regulations affecting naval service people. Sea time is sea time. It would be uncharitable, though none the less obvious, to suggest that the English language is being manipulated to reverse the first principle of clear and precise communication. The intellectual exercise of deliberate imprecision is a convenient means of maintaining an amorphous policy as difficult to pin down as an economist on a bad day. Notwithstanding the fact that in 1993 the DND minister and deputy minister admitted that service criteria was different for military veterans and merchant navy war veterans, the situation remains flawed.

Last year I was advised by a master mariner who had taken part in discussions with VAC officials that the anomalies were being corrected and by early 1995 my questions would be answered with positive action. I have not been able to contact my informant since that time and he has not called me. There seems to be an element among some senior members of the Canadian Merchant Navy Veterans Association that is very much impressed by contact with ministers, their deputies, and other bureaucrats. On more than one occasion, I have heard them speak about having lunch with the minister or meeting with the deputy and noting their cordial reception. It would be ungracious to criticize friendly hospitality on the part of anyone, yet there is the nagging doubt about whether social courtesies result in anything positive. There are those among us perhaps who are reassured by protocol and the heady atmosphere of ceremony.

I recall the irony of a naval engineer commander on a two-day cruise out of Halifax aboard one of our aircraft carriers. Early in 1950, a group of media people were invited to cover a show-the-flag expedition for a U.S.–Canada commission with General MacNaughton as host. After a demonstration of fly-off and safe landing of our aircraft on the carrier, we returned to port and on entering the harbour the crewmen had fallen in on the flight deck in traditional courtesy. Up harbour, the carrier was nudged into her berth at the Dockyard by tugs while we sat below in the engineer commander's cabin partaking of an end-of-voyage drink. The stamp of a hundred boots pounded on the flight deck overhead as our host poured. He looked up briefly. "Well, just time for a quick dram before they're finished there with their bullshit and gaiters." The commander shared the mild disdain of deck people and all their ways, an attitude rather common among marine engineers whose principal interest was the tone and efficiency of their propulsion machinery.

It is apparent that some merchant veterans, only a very few of our comrades, are more than impressed by pomp and circumstance. This is never more evident than during reunions or public memorial occasions when lengthy introductions of distinguished guests and rather superfluous ceremonies take place before getting down to immediate business. Dignified ceremony on notable occasions is to be commended, yet it frequently causes delay and confusion when specific matters are to be dealt with. It would take a generous leap of logic to understand the regard held by some CMNVA members for the Royal Canadian Legion, an organization that has consistently opposed not only equal recognition for merchant navy war veterans but in actual fact encouraged negative attitudes among the public. More than one Legion member, while in his cups to some degree, has suggested that our people only went to sea for high pay, that our crews were undisciplined, that we did not wear uniforms, and were perhaps little more than reluctant oafs forced aboard ship by latter-day press gangs. The majority of members who regard merchant mariners as deserving veterans are embarrassed by the discriminatory policies of their national command. It is not overseas veterans who support such reactionary policies, nor the large body of non-voting associate and auxiliary members who are faithful workers in the Legion's commendable public programs for youth and the disadvantaged.

The Legion now seems less aware of the dedicated and constructive policies inherent in its founding throughout the British Empire. Somewhere during the decades following the Second World War, some less enlightened Legion members began to develop inflated views of the organization's influence in the community, the province, and the nation. It was and continues to be an attitude much favoured by those aspiring to public office, who have a noticeable fondness for voters uncomfortable at the prospect of social change. A basic principle in the little notebook studied by ambitious candidates is a list of organizations to be treated with overt respect, no matter if their policies are ill-founded, unfair, or invidious, listened to carefully and quietly ignored through polite lip-service. A second principle in the little book advises the wisdom of silence or at the very least avoidance of commitment that may be interpreted as for or against. A regiment of wordsmiths is employed by political and special interest groups across the land to glorify the indefinite.

It is reluctant commentary to observe that there are a goodly number of indolent groups in this country and that in itself may be a reflection on the unavoidable aspects of current society. The knee-jerk tendency of reflex opposition to anything that seems, however gently, to rock the comfortable boat may go back to medieval times when God's will decreed things as they were, a view enforced by scripture and blade. The semi-medieval mind-set may be observed in the tone of correspondence. In a letter to the mayor of Ottawa on October 8, 1994, an official of the Royal Canadian Legion's Dominion Command responded to an enquiry sent to the mayor by the president of the Canadian Merchant Navy Veterans Association. It concerned merchant navy representation in the vice-regal group for the 1994 Remembrance Day national ceremony at the cenotaph in our capital city. The response to any queries regarding the presence of a merchant navy representative in the vice-regal group at the national ceremony was:

"The Royal Canadian Legion has organized the National Remembrance Ceremony in Ottawa since the end of World War I. It has always been the intent of the ceremony to provide one single annual occasion for the remembrance of Canada's 114,000 war dead regardless of service affiliation, race, religion, or any other circumstance. This obligation was to ensure that all veterans would be treated fairly and equally.

"To achieve equality and ensure equal treatment for all, the standard program devised has always provided the opportunity for all veterans groups and associations to participate on the same basis without regard to any of the aforementioned or other factors. This includes the protocols in wreath laying and the parade at the end of the ceremony where all veterans march in one group. The cooperation of the vice-regal group has not changed in years to ensure equality."

In the Legion letter, although not included in the statement of policy which is on a separate page, there is this comment:

"The vice-regal group lays wreaths in a designated order. This group is followed by representatives of specific veterans groups and military-associated organizations and the diplomatic corps groups. This is then followed by wreath laying by any other organization or individual that may wish to pay respects to Canada's war dead."

The "specific veterans groups and military-associated organizations" appear to exclude in practice, if not in principle, merchant marine veterans, while the diplomatic corps precedes any other organization or individual wishing to pay respects to war dead. Protocol to be observed and all bases covered. To quote again from the Legion's policy statement:

"The Merchant Navy, on the occasion of the unveiling of their Book of Remembrance, will join the vice-regal group for the laying of wreaths. This arrangement is to be for 1994 only and it is sincerely hoped that other veterans groups and organizations will understand this one-time departure from the standard practice."

What the official did not acknowledge was the Legion's objection to placement of the merchant marine Book of Remembrance in the Peace Tower on Remembrance Day, preferring Battle of the Atlantic Sunday in May. Some Members of Parliament interceded on our behalf and also asked that merchant seamen representatives be part of the official party to lay a wreath in memory of their war dead. The Legion agreed with some reluctance and only on condition it be on this occasion only. That threatening cloud called precedent is never far removed from the establishment whether civilian or military. In his concluding paragraphs the official defines the Legion's continuing policy:

"Whatever may happen as this matter progresses, in 1995, the Legion will continue to resist moves to alter the program (National Remembrance Day observances in Ottawa) in the interest of equality of representation of veterans in general and the practicality of attempting to satisfy all. The Legion maintains that at this national ceremony equality for all those who died and those who survived is a principle and a trust that cannot be broken lest someone be forgotten."

Lest someone be forgotten indeed! We have observed the deliberate forgetfulness of various organizations, including the Canadian government for half a century.

The Legion letter continues:

"It is hoped that any action taken [on representation at the national observances] will be on the side of equality for those who fought for that ideal in three wars and numerous missions around the world."

We may ask the precise definition of equality from the Legion's viewpoint. Is exclusion of merchant navy veterans from representation beside the navy, the army, and the air force anything less than blatant discrimination? Merchant seamen veterans wear medals too, not handed out with the rations, but justly earned without exception by *voluntary* service to the Allies on hostile seas. The Legion official's self-serving rhetoric is richly illuminated by a statement enunciated earlier in the letter to Ottawa's mayor: "The Legion is not an affiliation of any particular type of veteran and has members from every component from the Canadian veteran population." One wonders if those members include the large number of associates, whose qualifications vary greatly; the significant characteristic is that through no fault of their own they have not served in a war zone during years of conflict. To paraphrase George Orwell: All veterans are equal but some veterans are more equal than others.

Government policies have generally reflected the regressive attitude toward the merchant service exhibited by the Royal Canadian Legion, again principally its leadership. Other veterans organizations are less than receptive to the idea of equal veterans status for wartime seamen. It could be called an executive attitude that is certainly not shared by members who have served their sea time on the North Atlantic or on distant seas. The so-called Consultation Group, comprising the Legion, the National Coalition on Veterans Affairs, and the Army, Navy, Air Force Association, is considered the spokesperson for the merchant navy. That less-than-enlightened body, representing armed services veterans, has been unequivocally against the granting of equality to merchant veterans or their inclusion under the War Veterans Allowance Act. They endorsed the Merchant Navy Veterans and Civilian War-Related Benefits Act, which continues to regard us as civil veterans, a bureaucratic obfuscation. To be repetitive to the point of nausea, we have not received full veteran status, but the government's carefully orchestrated public relations effort gives the general public the impression that recognition for merchant navy service is at last enshrined in law.

The Con Group has consistently maintained that it supports our position, while approving legislation that may be described as fancy footwork that does not bear close examination. Words are a cheap commodity and can be used for more than common courtesy and the honest statement of reality. For many years our government claimed that Canadian veterans were the best cared for in the world. That was undeniably true for the deserving men and women who qualified as veterans under policies in effect at the time. That claim has now been modified to "Canadian veterans are *among* the best cared for in the world." The question expressed by a professor of history, Foster Griezic, asks: "By whose standards, with whom are the comparisons being made?" Obviously merchant navy wartime veterans are not included in the assumption; for half a century we have been among the most successfully ignored. It is curious yet understandable that the various military service organizations passively accept and parrot the government's practice of repeating ad infinitum the statement that we have been given full veterans status in the conviction that if something is repeated often enough, no matter how incorrect, it will be accepted by the general public as the revealed truth.

Military service organizations have supported a succession of veterans affairs ministers in their calculated efforts to perpetuate discrimination. With government encouragement military veterans organized the Con Group and refused to allow merchant seamen's representatives to take part in the consultative process. Significantly, merchant navy representatives were not permitted to see the draft bill before its presentation to parliament. That privilege was unique to the Con Group. The bill was intended, among other things, according to VAC, to extend "equality" to our group. Only the military service representatives had an opportunity to review the draft legislation. As it happens, the omissions, confusions and fallacious terminology, if seen beforehand in draft form, would have raised strong objections from merchant navy veterans. None were expressed by those purporting to represent our interests. As someone has said recently about the government of a far eastern nation: "They do not wish to control elections, they just want to know the result beforehand."

Naive trust in declared political intentions over the years and inexperience in dealing with public information about the Canadian Merchant Navy Veterans Association has contributed to muddying the waters. Senior civil servants, as principal advisers to cabinet ministers, exhibit a flawed sense of recent history and a severe lack of analytical scholarship. I am reluctant to observe that some people in my own trade of journalism are less than perceptive in their conclusions.

Frontenac Park
Built at Sorel, Quebec in 1944, the *Frontenac Park* was renamed *Victoria County* in 1946, then *Akron* in 1950. Russell Latimer of Dartmouth, Nova Scotia sailed in her as radio operator for two years on thirty voyages carrying United Nations Refugee Agency and Marshall Plan cargoes to post-war Europe. She was scrapped in Japan in 1965. (Photo: Wetmore Photo, Maritime Museum of the Atlantic, N-23067)

Halifax, May 7, 1945

Trouble in the streets; senior officers of the Armed Forces and the Royal Canadian Mounted Police were in a state of panic approaching low-grade catalepsy. Mayor Allan Butler feared the worst: civil disobedience, perhaps bloodshed. Had he the authority, he would have declared martial law. He tried to get the services and police to act, but when a decision came it was too late. Instead, the Halifax population viewed theft and destruction of property that one observer likened to the town being captured and plundered by a horde of vandals. It was a scene of devastation with broken glass and empty bottles strewn along the streets. In brief, naval authorities allowed personnel to leave their duties or stand-by status to go ashore, a term which applied even to the Dockyard which was already ashore. The estimated cost of losses and damage to the small city rang in at $5 million, a not inconsequential sum at a time when bread cost fifteen cents a loaf and cigarettes one cent each.

The army and air force were under discipline. Even if not controlled, soliders and airmen were not inclined to vent their anger, if any, on the community or citizens who had to exist under difficult conditions in a crowded city. Crews of navy ships tied up at the Dockyard remained aboard. Barely more than a handful of those men went ashore to find fun and destruction. There are indications that most troublemakers were shore staff angry at what they felt was price gouging by merchants and landlords. There were no civilian taverns, while naval ratings had wet canteens to heal their thirst. Civilians were under rationing and could buy one case of beer and one bottle of spirits per month; their sale was registered on an identity card stamped to prevent additional purchases until the first day of the following month.

The booze complaint was one aspect of the anger building to the point where rumours spread that the end of the war in Europe would be a rough day for Halifax. There is some reason to think of these complainers as cry-babies. Many were far from home and living in uncomfortable conditions. Overseas, many thousands of Canadians were neck-deep in the watery flatlands of the Low Countries after front-line service in Italy, from Sicily to the Alps, through Normandy and into the Rhineland. Thousands more had been flying or maintaining fighter aircraft and bombers since the Battle of Britain five years earlier and across the broken fields of Europe.

Much of the blame for the wholesale looting and destruction can be laid at the doorstep of the navy's introductory training, or lack of it. They had to ready recruits for service as quickly as possible. Even so, it doesn't take weeks to instil a sense of responsibility, rather than encourage feelings of arrogant superiority, in disciplined army and air force personnel; suspicions of draft-evasion or profiteering dogged civilians. Many of us had been rejected for military service, Cateogry E which roughly translated meant the lame, the halt, and the visually challenged. We had volunteered for the merchant marine, knowing that every man aboard was a volunteer. Keep in mind, we could have remained safely ashore of no use to the military. We learned marine discipline and respect for masters and mates, all professional mariners. The absence of indoctrination in appropriate conduct and respect for the uniform a man wears is not a new development. During the inquiry into the Halifax Riots of May 7-8, 1945, revealing evidence of this problem was cited as an excuse for losing control of service people.

Many months earlier the tough-minded managing editor of the *Halifax Herald* was furious at what he saw as the failure of the Commander-in-Chief, Northwest Atlantic, Rear-Admiral Murray, to enforce discipline in Halifax. The editor complained directly to the navy's Chief of Staff, Vice-Admiral Jones. Bob Rankin's letter to the Chief of Naval Staff was mailed in 1944; Captain Connolly was sent down from Ottawa to investigate. And little wonder!

The editor stated his main purpose:

"in writing at this time was to bring to your attention a situation which, if not corrected, might become exceedingly serious.

"It has to do with the shore activities of the Royal Canadian Navy which have lately become sufficiently objectionable to bring forth considerable public complaint and a substantial demand that newspapers should have something to say about the matter on behalf of the people of the community.

"I do not suggest that the Navy personnel generally are at fault. I confidently believe that the trouble-making element would be no more than say three to five per cent, but that is sufficient to create a difficult situation. With a number of protests before me, I took the liberty of requesting the Public Relations Officer and the Shore Patrol Officer to attend an informal conference. ... We had received complaints regarding the public use of obscene language, the attitude of sailors toward unescorted women on the streets and, in some instances, definite protests about the openly indecent actions of men wearing Naval uniforms. Further, I would call to your attention the fact that damage to property is becoming more expensive. It is surprising to note the number of store fronts in the downtown area after the windows have been broken on numerous occasions.

"The two officers advised me that they regretted that there did not seem that anything could be done. I pointed out that the same difficulty did not seem to exist with regard to either the Air Force or the Army."

Mr. Rankin went on to say in his letter that he received a call from the mayor of Halifax advising that one Captain Armstrong had heard the *Herald* proposed to publish a provocative article and the navy did not plan to accept responsibility for what might happen following publication.

With the convening of the Royal Commission of Inquiry into the Halifax Riots, the picture of mismanagement and inertia became clear. The inquiry, under Mr. Justice Kellock of the Supreme Court of Canada, convened in the Legislative Chamber of Province House in Halifax. From the beginning of testimony it was obvious that authority was divided to say the least and the line of command was clogged by inertia and pre-conceived opinions. Senior officers of the three Armed Forces and the City of Halifax had conferred on means of maintaining order in the community when VE Day arrived. Unfortunately, most of the difficulty arose from ill-informed direction on the part of the naval commander, Admiral Murray. He testified that only about two hundred ratings had taken part in the rioting, adding that he was under the impression that civilians were leading the mob, and service personnel followed them. No effort was made to reinforce shore patrols which were thin in number compared to the total population of naval personnel.

In the Halifax area the army had 169 security personnel for its forty-five hundred members on leave on VE Day. The RCAF had 194 service police for duty in Halifax-Dartmouth and advised the mayor that all available personnel had been called out. The air force complement on leave in the area was 3,330. When it was reported that a mob had attacked Keith's Brewery, RCAF personnel were ordered confined to barracks. The navy in its home port of Halifax had, according to the admiral, 267 shore patrol on duty. It was estimated that 9,000 navy men were on leave, excused from duty, and a large number of them were in the city's relatively small downtown area. During the inquiry it became obvious that the navy was clutching at straws in trying to downplay involvment of its personnel in the rioting and destruction. Admiral Murray admitted as much in his statement to the press on May 9, 1945, when he said civilians had led the assault on Keith's Brewery. He had been told by his house steward that only about fifteen navy men had been involved. Murray reiterated that he was under the impression that civilians were leading the mob and service personnel followed.

Mr. Justice Kellock asked: "Nine thousand went on leave and you have a belief that a smaller number went down town and only a small number of ratings took part in the disturbances. Upon what did you base that belief?"

The admiral responded: "I had no exact information. I'm trying to recall. Would it help you any if I were to say that it was a comparatively small number?"

Mr. Justice Kellock reminded him that he had said two hundred. If only two hundred ratings were engaged, he asked why, if 237 Shore Patrol could not handle them, were reinforcements not sent.

Murray responded: "I thought that any interference would have caused bloodshed between sailors and civilians."

The admiral's statement issued on May 9 by navy public relations said in part: "I am satisfied that though service personnel were present during the whole of the afternoon (May 8), in almost all cases, particularly in the looting of Keith's Brewery, and the orgy of window-breaking along Barrington Street, civilians led the assault and encouraged service personnel to take part."

One is tempted to shed a tear for the poor innocent lads enticed into evil ways by civilians. Admiral Murray had something to say on that point. He testified that he had been told "that three civilians led the way at the brewery where the sailors were being guided away from it by the Shore Patrol. ... I am unable to recall who told me." Some time later, journalist Hugh Garner, an ex-navy man, wrote in a magazine article on the Halifax riots that three merchant seamen had shoved a flagpole through the window of the Sackville Street liquor store. Was this an expansive exaggeration based on the Admiral's comment even though the Admiral was unable to recall who told him?

The Halifax riots represented a sad chapter in the history of the Royal Canadian Navy, but even more shameful are continuing efforts to blame the City of Halifax and its citizens for their heartless attitude toward naval personnel. One would hope that navy men did not expect comfortable hometown conditions to exist in a community with its wartime population doubled by service personnel and civilian workers engaged in essential port and supply activities. Halifax harbour and vicinity were under half-blackout regulations during the war years. From time to time submarines armed with torpedoes as well as acoustic mine-laying subs were hardly a cannon shot off Chebucto Head. The personal comfort and convenience of individual service personnel was not high on the priority list. Such amenities were rarely available in theatres of war far from our shores.

The naval commander was preoccupied with the defence of the vital convoy base and the prime minister was aware of the concern. Mr. King wrote to Winston Churchill in March 1941, asking that Halifax and strategic approaches be given special protection. King wrote, "... in particular the importance of adequate protection for the convoy assembly port of Halifax and strategic approaches cannot be too strongly emphasized. We should be very glad to have your views on the situation and to learn whether, having in mind the requirements of the various theatres of war, it will be possible to strengthen these features of our home defence position which Chiefs of Staff analysis has shown to be inadequate." The response from Winston Churchill: "The position is bluntly that we have not all the equipment that would enable us to give complete protection on both sides of the Atlantic, and the question is therefore how can we make the best use of material we have, having regard to what the enemy is trying to do and probabilities as to his future course of action? If we were to divert any substantial part of our defences from this present area of operations to cover wider areas where there is admittedly some risk of enemy action, we should only imperil the whole and play into his hands."

Mr. King was not alone in his lack of comprehension. Could incompetence at lower levels of authority lead to the breakdown of naval discipline at war's end and the subsequent rioting and destruction of property in Halifax? Admiral Murray assumed full responsibility for that regrettable situation, yet he had carried a heavy burden and had to depend on an indecisive senior staff that ignored portents of possible disciplinary problems when the war came to an end. The inquiry revealed as well that the command system was poorly organized. Regardless of causes, the fact remains that those in authority did not appreciate the possible dangers of a collapse in discipline and failure to observe appropriate service conduct for those in the King's uniform. Certainly, a large majority, if not ninety-five per cent of the uniformed rioters, were personnel on various shore duties. Men with much sea time aboard corvettes and frigates were largely absent from the riotous activites of VE Day. It brings to mind the comment by Charles Edward Montague, "War hath no fury like a non-combatant." At various times during the inquiry navy witnesses deftly dropped suggestions that the ratings had been led on by the civilian population. The question arises: would police have tolerated widespread looting and property destruction if there had been no service people in the streets to celebrate VE Day?

Four weeks after the Halifax riot, a deplorable incident occurred in the far Pacific where Allied naval forces were clearing the sea approaches to Japan in preparation for the final assault and invasion of the home islands. The eventual destruction of Hiroshima and Nagasaki by the atom bomb remained locked in secrecy at the highest levels. Aboard the cruiser *HMCS Uganda*, Captain Rollo

Mainguy and his staff followed instructions from the Canadian government to hold a referendum to identify volunteers for the Pacific theatre. The MacKenzie King government's declared policy was that only volunteers would serve in the closing campaign against Japan. On June 3, 1945, Captain Mainguy's staff set up three ballot boxes on the cruiser's quarterdeck, one for the federal election to be held in July, the second for the Ontario provincial election on June 4. The third ballot box was for the Pacific volunteer referendum. The result is significant. Of the nine hundred who voted, three hundred volunteered, six hundred elected not to serve in the Pacific theatre, voting to abandon the war in the midst of an unfinished campaign. That decision, which amounted to individual, personal and certainly deliberate dereliction of moral purpose, was to walk away from their declared commitment, taking the opportunity provided by a wimpish administration with entirely political motives.

For the three hundred who volunteered for the Far East campaign, authorities in Ottawa were now required to honour their entitlement of thirty days home leave prior to reporting for duty in the Pacific theatre. No matter that the three hundred were at the moment of making the commitment already in western Pacific waters aboard *Uganda*, they had to be returned home first. The British Task Force (Pacific) pulled back for resupply in preparation for the expected invasion of the Japanese islands. It would resume strategic operations but without the contribution of the Canadian ship. *Uganda* left the South Pacific for Esquimalt. At the end of the journey she entered port in the dark hours, in silence and without cheers as one writer described the arrival: "... the only ship on record in naval history whose own company had, by majority, voted her out of the war." Commander Tony Gorman said in his book, *The Sea is at Our Gates, The History of the Canadian Navy*, that "volunteers in the RCN couldn't get out soon enough. Veterans preference gave them their jobs back if they wanted them and there were plenty of new ones in a buoyant economy, as well as free university courses and vocational training."

By contrast, merchant navy veterans were forbidden by law to apply for jobs ashore, a provision that stretched a year and a half into the postwar period. For the very few who defied the rules and made a pier-head jump either because of home responsibilities or to upgrade their skills, there was absolutely no assistance or encouragement from a benevolent government. There is no intention to deny the right of deserved benefits to uniformed veterans, but the distribution may be questioned. Wearing the King's uniform in honourable service certainly did not justify classification of individuals as having overseas service for a one-hour voyage by ferry across Northumberland Strait, between New Brunswick and Prince Edward Island, and to offer the same veterans the opportunity to pursue free college or vocational training. Conversely, in December 1944 a merchant ship was torpedoed in the Halifax harbour approaches. Hours later, two more merchant vessels were torpedoed off Egg Island, twenty miles east of the harbour. A couple of weeks later, three more cargo ships were torpedoed in thirteen minutes two miles east of Sambro Head. Their crews were not recognized as war veterans. At that time, the federal government was licking its chops over the possibility that the war would be over by the autumn of 1945. The conscription crisis could be forgotten, and the Liberal party returned to power in confirmation of divine authority revealed in MacKenzie King's crystal ball.

SS Canadian Victor
The *Canadian Victor*, a 4,700-ton cargo vessel built between the wars at Canadian Vickers shipyard in Montreal, served mainly in Canada's west coast waters in the Second World War.
(Wetmore Photo, Maritime Museum of the Atlantic, N-23,066)

Days at sea & death of a leader

The long days in convoy, often with minimal escort, were to be endured with the comforting routine of life at sea, your ship a tiny nation and alone. Endless days were filled with four-on, eight-off duty, without respite. On the many occasions when our cableship made its solitary way on a wide sea toward the position of a cable fault, there was an extra edge of apprehension. Sixty human beings on a small ship with nothing to be seen to the north, south, east, or west but wave tops and the gentle progress of sea mists on their errant course. It is the usual condition of seagong men in more peaceful times. Now war and the U-boat, the wolf fish unleashed from concrete caves in Bremerhaven, Germany or L'Orient on the coast of occupied France, changed all that. It is probable that half of our time at sea in the war years was without escort. We had no choice and went where ordered.

The journeys in convoy had the advantage of things to be observed and analyzed, time to ponder the cargoes being carried by the other-than-obvious tankers with their various grades of petroleum products from fuel oil to the volatile high-octane gasoline with its explosive potential of instant destruction. The problem was that we weren't told what tankers carried. Early on, we developed profound respect for anything that looked like a liquid fuel carrier.

That was especially true for those who had witnessed the detonation of a tanker torpedoed at anchor just off Sandy Hook, New Jersey. Pieces of steel dropped from the skies with the intensity of a tropical rain storm.

A twenty-six vessel convoy would have two to four escorts, again depending on awareness of submarine activity and availability of ships. The commodore or senior officer of the cargo vessels would be responsible for following various courses and visual communication with escort ships by flags or Aldis lamp. Their instructions were contained in a sealed envelope issued at the pre-sailing convoy conference at the Halifax Dockyard or other locations in departure ports. Merchant navy radio officers accompanied their shipmasters to the conference and were given a sealed envelope with radio signal information, special codes, call signs, etc. Sailing times were only communicated to the captains, who immediately gave them to the navigator as soon as they were back aboard to allow a fast start on corrections to the coastal charts and menaces to navigation that might be expected in various locations. These included the varying schedules for coastal lighthouses meant to confuse submarine captains who might expect teutonic consistency in orders to light up or extinguish marine beacons.

Some days earlier, the ship had been cleared for sea with an open departure date. The purser and radio operator had dallied for a moment to buy soap and matches for a voyage which could include weeks of lonely isolation circling a marker buoy while waiting for favourable weather to proceed with a cable repair, and often without escort and vulnerable to submarine attack if one happened by. In convoy there was visible protection. A convoy is a close formation of ships travelling in company with the advantage that its cohesive organization allows relatively efficient protection by escort vessels against hostile action. A small convoy of eight to twelve merchant ships of the size assigned to serve the St. John's, Halifax, Saint John, or Boston run would usually be escorted by a minesweeper armed with depth charges or from time to time a corvette, depending on availability.

Large convoys bound for the UK ports of Liverpool, Glasgow, or Southampton would have several corvettes or frigates in escort, and when the area was hot with the danger of submarine wolf packs, destroyers would accompany convoys on a wider circle. Merchant ships sailed in a horizontal line, port to starboard, and in vertical rows from the lead ship, aft, and ships following were numbered in sequence.

1st line	A	B	C	D	E
2nd line	2	2	2	2	2
3rd line	3	3	3	3	3
4th line	4	4	4	4	4
5th line	5	5	5	5	5
6th line		6	6	6	
7th line		7	7	7	

For example, if the master of the *Neversail* had been advised he was assigned to position C3, he knew he would be in the third line of the convoy and third in sequence. Once through the gate vessels and beyond the harbour approaches, the ships would proceed to take up their convoy position. With the exception of enemy attacks or very severe weather conditions, the convoy formation would be maintained until the necessary course alterations were made in preparation for entering the port of destination.

By regulation, a ship's international identification letters served as her radio call sign, although it was not to be used during the war even if radio silence had to be broken in an emergency such as torpedo attack. British and Canadian ships and other Allied vessels had been given new call signs. In fact, our ship, registered in London but operating out of Halifax and owned by Western Union of New York, enjoyed two of them: GW5NA from the Admiralty in the UK, and VI4UR issued by Ottawa in an apparent declaration of national sovereignty. MacKenzie King's people were touchy about our country's authority, as noted on later occasions, such as Mr.

King's annoyance that a carillon proposed for a bluff above the falls by the Niagara Falls Bridge Commission would be dedicated to "our nation's leaders, Churchill and Roosevelt." King complained to his Liberal party people that they should generate a nationwide protest. He said his party was led by a man who had carried six elections out of seven; it was, he also said, a reflection on the Canadian people as a whole.

Well now, here was our Canadian call sign and I was on the horns of a dilemma. The advisory from the Ministry of Transport did not bother to advise or suggest, even if they knew the difference, whether the United Kingdom call sign was to be set aside, nullified, abandoned, or used in tandem with VI4UR. For months I worried about what to do if our ship was torpedoed and I was ordered to send out the SSSS and our latitude and longitude as instructed by Allied shipping authorities. The four-letter signal identified the problem as submarine attack rather than other marine emergencies. Luckily it was a decision I never had to make. The closest we came to attack was in the dying hours of the war in of all places, Long Island Sound, a league off Point Judith, Rhode Island. I have since thought of what I could have done if the bridge had been put out of action and the Old Man and his officers hors de combat. How in the name of Davy Jones would I guess at our latitude and longitude to follow the SSSS? There would not have been time to check the position on the chart, even if I had one. I didn't know then we were close to Point Judith. The distress signal used shortly before the First World War was CQD, CQD, CQD, devised by adding D (for danger) to the CQ signal for calling all stations. The SOS came into use shortly after by international agreement for calling attention to any kind of emergency.

Nothing is as unforgiving as history, unless it is the product of those of us with the post-operative privilege of polishing up the positive and easing the uncomplimentary behind a convenient curtain. A latter-day Tale of Two Cities concerns two convoys recalled in some detail. The first, of which we were commodore ship, was bound from Boston to Halifax; we were headed north after many weeks in the Caribbean. Our ship was anchored in the outer harbour of Boston, while the Old Man and I went ashore to a convoy conference. After our meeting in the old Causeway Building on the Charles River and distribution of the sealed envelopes, the Old Man was advised in confidence that the convoy would not sail earlier than Friday. It was now Wednesday and the prospect of a day and a couple of evenings ashore was pleasant indeed. Outside we went to a tavern across from Boston Gardens and had food and drink. Bill looked at me under his bushy white eyebrows, his pale blue eyes more introspective than usual. "You have relatives here, or others to visit perhaps?"

"Yes sir, one of the Boston harbour pilots, Stan Balcom, is from Port Dufferin. I know him well. In fact, I have a forty-ouncer of good rum for him if I have time to visit in Rochester."

The Old Man smirked. "Fine then, this is Wednesday so meet me here at ten sharp Friday morning. Now we go our separate, happy ways. As I recall Scollay Square is in that direction, perhaps a nostalgic visit to the Old Howard is in order."

With that, dismissed and free, I called Stan's house and proceeded by civic transport to Rochester where I was welcomed by Stan and Ralda. They invited some cousins and friends for a down-home reunion. I was pleased my gift for him was warmly received with profound thanks and stowed out of range of the guests. He said that good Demerara rum just out of the keg deserved personal attention and he would retain it for home use specifically. But other liquid refreshment was available. Ralda cooked remarkable food in a time of rationing, and we had a happy gathering in their family room downstairs. Next day, awake betimes, as Ben Franklin that Old Bostonian would say, then more partying. On Friday morning early, Stan shook me awake. As I pulled on my shore-going pants and jacket, he poured coffee and presented waffles, sausage, and maple syrup: all tasteful but requiring effort to overcome the searing hangover endemic to Rochester. We drove in his sta-

93

tion wagon toward the waterfront. As we passed through Scollay Square and its five converging streets, as it was in those days, I wondered if the Old Man had enjoyed his sojourn ashore. What? The *Boston Globe* says it's Saturday; am I a day late and adrift? The Old Man would keel-haul me. Stan dropped me off with a good-luck wave. I walked down the pier to the security office and was offered a cup of coffee. I sat down to wait for the duty boat and listened to the conversation of Charlie and his helper. They were talking about the visit by Putzi Haenfstengl, the German pianist and pet of Adolf Hitler, who had attended the twenty-fifth reunion of his Harvard class some years earlier.

Charlie had been a Boston cop and when City Hall was asked by the German embassy to provide security for Putzi while he was at his Harvard reunion, appropriate action was taken. Sergeant Greenberg assigned senior men from the vice-squad to accompany the Harvard grad at all times. According to Charlie, they were two very large and mean detectives named Klein and Meyer who spent their time in the background hoping that somebody would throw a bomb at the Nazi piano player. It didn't happen, but Charlie said the chances of their intervening in an assasination attempt was slim, to say the least. Just as the story was progressing, a taxi drew up outside the door. I looked out and saw the Old Man opening the back door and getting out, slowly as if he was not functioning on all cylinders. I went out and he greeted me cheefully. I didn't dare tell him it was now Saturday and we were a day late. We went out to the ship on the next water taxi and went up the ladder; the chief officer was on deck looking worried.

"Where have you been, sir? The Coast Guard said you hadn't reported in at the Causeway Building and had a warrant out for both of you."

The Old Man wasn't very concerned. "We were at the conference; that's Coast Guard efficiency for you, isn't it. Are we ready to sail and is the pilot aboard? If so, let's go."

The chief officer ordered up anchor and five minutes later with the captain on the bridge we proceeded out of the harbour, and one by one ships of the convoy followed us out past the examination station. We sailed into open water and northeast well clear of Cape Cod on course to the Sambro Lightship off Halifax. I was in the radio shack looking through the convoy fact sheet and digesting the information. The date of departure was wrong. Perhaps I'd better advise the Old Man. But he was busy sleeping off his shoreside exertions. What we didn't know and no one told us was that the convoy's departure had been postponed until Sunday. We were under way twenty-four hours early and nobody seemed to notice. I suppose the Coast Guard was reluctant to mention the matter now that we were at sea. The security station had apparently regarded our departure as merely a change in orders. It seems a small matter after all these years. One senior officer suggested that the only person interested in the event was the spy who dutifully passed on the Saturday departure time of convoy BH47 to his contact man.

If it makes anyone feel more secure, the other side made errors in judgment as well but few people knew about them until after the war. On another occasion, the convoy routing officer, or someone on his staff, ordered our group of ships out of Halifax right into a fog bank rolling in past Thrumcap, just off the harbour entrance. Bad weather sailings were not uncommon, but this one had the added difficulty of being routed directly through an incoming convoy just breaking formation and proceeding up the approaches. For a couple of hours, the gentle swish of a quiet sea was broken by engine telegraph bells jangling harshly through the mist with orders of half-ahead, full-astern, punctuated by the shouted commands Hard Over or Midships to helmsmen. As far as anyone knew, ships had gotten in or out safely, depending on their inclination, with only superficial dents in their bow-plates and dignity.

Except for such rare incidents, convoy duty was almost never-ending tedium. We listened on the international distress frequency of 500 kilocycles for urgent messages and other channels for the call sign list of ships with traffic pending. Constant attention was required on watches, but with much leisure time sandwiched in there was opportunity to read, study, or meditate, always subject to immediate alert if required. My cabin was on the starboard side of the boat deck, in the same deckhouse as the radio room which opened to port. The wooden partition was easily penetrated by the sound of radio code messages over the loudspeaker, an improvement on the traditional earphones which used to provide wearers with wavy hair before it made them bald. In a strange way, I heard and mentally recorded the messages even while asleep. No need to read the messages when I relieved Jim at midnight, they were already in my head down to the last letter and comma. This electronic penetration of the skull luckily did not interfere with sleep, at sea nothing much does. When you are off-watch, you either eat, play cards, or sleep at any opportunity.

Aside from my duties as assistant purser, which included typing the lengthy logs of cable repair operations, the eight hours a day on-watch were fairly free other than to listen closely to broadcast signals. After a time, listening became a habit that would become a lifetime practice. There was plenty of time to fill and insufficient books to read. The ship's library was renewed as often as possible, but space was limited and the money available from the booze profit of the officers mess was not limitless. Prices of the duty-free purser's delight were deliberately kept low by majority vote of members. I decided early on to increase my modest level of knowledge and enrolled in an electrical engineering correspondence course with ICS at Scranton, Pennsylvania. It was the ideal college atmosphere without the nuisance of lecturers or argumentative teachers. There would be enough of them when your exam papers went through the mill of the engineering desk in ICS's headquarters. The school had a wide reputation for excellence which spilled over on many of its alumnae, present company excepted.

Another of my tasks was to write the daily newspaper. Because of the danger of re-radiation from ordinary radio receivers being picked up by submarines in the vicinity to give them a position fix, the use of private receivers was forbidden by regulation on Allied vessels. All ships, regardless of flag, were required to carry communication equipment certified to be free of re-radiation. Seamen, from master to deck-boy, had a personal interest in daily events and particularly in the conduct of the war at sea. We were in it, but not of it, unless someone snapped a torpedo at us or our neighbour in a convoy. That was about it. With full censorship, it seemed only the enemy's English-language broadcasts mentioned specifics and who knew if they were telling the truth. The uses of propaganda are wide and not confined to the good guys or the bad.

The task of writing a daily paper of five or six pages, double-spaced on the old Underwood typewriter was difficult at first but was the best training possible in analyzing news sources for a scattering of truth behind the hyperbole. When one realized that a strategic redeployment of forces indicated a retreat, the first step had been made in the journalist's trade: "It might be true, but we'll confirm when we get the facts verified by an impartial source." So, how to entertain the crew without being cynical? The answer: tell them what you can and let them make up their own minds. It's a policy less widely emulated in these so-called days of enlightenment. Some of the many items written about included the daily review of where our ship was a year earlier:

"One year ago today, our ship lay at Vera Cruz in Mexico where we awaited orders from New York to proceed to repair work in the Gulf. Shore leave included a visit by some of our crew to a bullfight which was interesting and sobering to those who had never seen the slaughter of innocent animals before their eyes." That story was timely indeed, the afternoon after the bullfight, food supplies were delivered to the pier in a horse-drawn wagon, and a calf tagged along behind the vehicle at rope's end. On arrival, the chandler's helper grasped the calf's slender neck under his left arm and cut its throat; it collapsed twitching on the concrete pier and the assistant proceeded with butchering at what modern suppliers would call the point of sale. Tough old deck hands and fire-men watched the event with pale faces. For some time, the chief steward avoided referring to veal on the menu, preferring to list the dinner as Baltimore stew. Such events, while important to the calf, were the perfunctory kind of stories which our crew seemed to like. They related to honest seagoing folk, or so they thought. Some of the other stuff was creative to the point of blatant fabrication.

But there were days of sadness or grief for the loss of a leader who had earned confidence and was already one of the pil-lars of history. In April of 1945 we were off Cape Hatteras, destina-tion New York. A few of us had just finished dinner, including the Old Man who had come in late to join the chief engineer and other senior officers, taking his place at the head of number one table. We juniors were at the other table, listening to the conversation of our elders; we seldom entered such discussions and then only if asked a direct question from the High Table, as we referred to it. The ship's doctor was usually first at meals and the first to finish. He said he was used to eating on the run over forty years in coun-try medical practice when he often left knife and fork in mid-air to hasten to a patient downed by accident or sudden and severe ill-ness.

Dr. Rommell had left the saloon a few minutes earlier and gone to his cabin to pick up the news on his new radio, certified as radiation free and safe for use. Although the war was winding down, submarines were still about off New England and the Maritimes and the southeast coast of the United States. On that voyage our only escort was one of the US Navy blimps on regular patrol along the hundred-fathom line, delineating the charted depth of water along that portion of the continental shelf. The saloon door opened suddenly and the doctor entered. We looked up at his shocked expression. "Sir, gentlemen, I've just heard on the radio that President Roosevelt died this afternoon!" There was a sudden hush, even the young steward paused on his way to the saloon pantry with plates and cups, as if frozen in his place. The Old Man, who had been through two wars, seemed to be shaken by the news. We expected him to say what we were all thinking; he did. "Gentlemen, we've lost one of the great men of our time." He cleared his throat and turned to the chief officer. "Scotty, order the flag to half staff. And, if you will allow me fifteen minutes to make arrangements, you all are invited to join me for a toast to the late FDR." The Old Man glanced toward the sods table. "Unless you younger men have urgent duties, please come along."

Our master was not an emotional man, vitriolic seemed a more appropriate description of his usual response to circumstances that interfered with the measured and comfortable routine of his days. After some years, I came to understand that anger was a smokescreen for an able and often lonely man. He was a widower with a son at school in England and living with his grandmother, a Labour Member of Parliament. An invitation to share a glass in his day cabin was a rare event, something like entering a sanctuary, one most appropriate to mourning a man of courage and principle whose memory would stand with that of Lincoln. When we gathered in the day cabin, the Old Man stood behind the rather small mahogany table on which a tray of glasses was placed together with bottles of Havana Club rum, single-malt Scotch from the misty western isles, and London Dry gin for those born within the sound of Bow Bells.

Waving the steward aside, the Old Man poured the booze personally; he really wanted to make this ceremony his own contribution to the memory of a great leader with the qualities of universal man. To understand the discipline of the merchant service, the regard in which a respected and admired man was held, it might help to consider the observation of an able-bodied seaman who said to me, "Old Bill sure knows his trade, and understands his people. There may be more skippers around like him, but damned few I'd think." I had some understanding of the other side of the coin from day-to-day work in the purser's office. Captain Adamson had a very high regard for the quality of his crew, although he would sometimes growl that our seamen and stewards were better dressed for going ashore than many of the officers. With all glasses charged, he raised his drink: "Gentlemen, older shipmates and the young lads who joined us during the war, it is a privilege to call for a farewell toast to Franklin Delano Roosevelt." We drank, and the steward picked up our glasses and returned them to the tray. "And now we'll have a social drink," the captain said and poured again, carefully, with his tongue stuck out as it did when he was sawing away at his violin.

He spoke as he poured, "Well, if we can get through another few months, we'll have survived another war and I must admit it's getting a bit weary. It's thirty years since I chipped paint as apprentice boy on the Hungry Hogarth line." He handed the first glass to Norman Richardson Douglass, a Tynesider. "Mr. Chief Engineer, your comments please." Bill winked at old Doug and I suspected they shared many a dram of malt whisky in their quiet hours. The chief cleared his throat, "Thank you, sir, and I want to echo your thoughts about old comrades and the young lads who served with us the past few years. We Englishmen are rather shy at first, but after a few years we can say more than good morning, eh boys. In the North Country where I come from they will certainly say: ' 'e were a good lad,' and that is just what I say to all of you, you're the best of lads."

Now it was back to work, to the routine of four-on, eight-off and the two-hour dog-watches that kept the rotation in order so we continued on the same sequence. Except for the dog-watches, my time in the shack was twelve to four, beginning at noon and again at midnight, seven days a week while at sea, off-watch at four a.m. in the bright light of summer dawn, and the privilege of sleeping until noon every day.

SS Liverpool Loyalist
A general cargo carrier, prior to 1942 the *Liverpool Loyalist* was the *Zenda*. Built in 1932 at Wallsend, UK, by Swan, Hunter and Wisham Richardson Ltd., she was owned by the Liverpool Loyalist Shipping Co. Ltd. (Photo: Maritime Museum of the Atlantic, Halifax, NS #8902)

SS Nerissa in the "Narrows," St. John's, Newfoundland
The *Nerissa*, with a gross tonnage of 5,553, was built in 1926 by William Hamilton & Co. of the United Kingdom. Owned by the New York, Newfoundland and Halifax Steamship Company, she was torpedoed and sunk in April 1941 with heavy loss of life. (Photo: Maritime Museum of the Atlantic, N11,284)

Yesterday's children

How many children, boys of twelve, thirteen, fourten, fifteen years of age, went to sea on merchant vessels from schooners to cargo ships during the Second World War? That is a serious question, but will remain simply a rhetorical inquiry. There are reasons, many of them, why these boys, now old men, left home. First was the stifling poverty of communities in the dreary months and years of the Depression. That led to a desire on the part of young minds to make a little money and send some home to help mum and younger brothers and sisters. The chance to join a ship as a deck boy or galley slave meant a narrow bunk to sleep in, regular meals, and money for cigarettes (ten cents for a pack of twenty) and eight or ten dollars a month to send home. I know about these things because as assistant purser it was my task to see that the money was deducted at our shore office and mailed back to the distant coves or coastal hamlets of Newfoundland and the Maritime provinces.

The reason why we will never know the approximate number of underaged seamen in the war years is the lack of records and information. First, in Newfoundland, vessels under fifty tons burden were not required to have ship's articles (the contractual documents which declare business, personnel, and legal obligations of a ship's operation). The reality is that many of these relatively small carriers transported food, general supplies, fuel, and some military items from major Atlantic coast ports to the small communities and Armed Forces locations from Labrador, the Gulf of St. Lawrence, and Newfoundland waters to the Bay of Fundy. As I write this, I am looking at a chart with positions of the scores of ships sunk by German submarines in those waters; it was not safe territory. Newfoundland shipping records presented a further complication. It may be the result of more detailed research still to be done, or as is the case in Ottawa, the diffusion of civilian shipping records through various offices or agencies of government. Things do get confused, not because of deliberate neglect but also perhaps due to the tangled lines of custodial responsibility as departments merged or reorganized.

The nucleus of the problem is, of course, in the system, or lack of system, in the ports or districts responsible for such records, if in fact they were given that responsibility in the first place. Jurisdictions or lines of authority do change under unusual circumstances. In the early 1930s, the Newfoundland economy was in a state of collapse and the Colonial Office in London was asked to establish and maintain a so-called Commission of Government to run the island's affairs. In effect, it was rule by fiat, albeit with the historical benevolence of Great Britain toward its former colonies. The result was disenfranchisement of the population while the commission began its task of rejuvenation, which would be achieved to some degree by the advent of war, a situation similar to its influence on Canada's Maritime provinces.

The state of Newfoundland's marine records is illustrated by the story of a man who sailed as a child of twelve on a small schooner and a second vessel from 1942 to 1944. This man is now sixty-six. His birthdate was November 11, 1929, as verified by his baptismal certificate. He now lives on the south shore of Nova Scotia and I omit his full name because his claim for benefit recognition, rejected by three levels of government, may be appealed to the federal cabinet. Malcolm consulted with his lawyer and in 1987 made his original application for a Civilian War Allowance, and subsequently, when it came into effect, the Merchant Navy Veterans Allowance. His claim was rejected by the Veterans Affairs regional office, appealed to the Atlantic Regional Departmental Adjudicator, and the Veteran's Appeal Board of Canada. The appeal board's decision came on February 18, 1992. I was shown the documentation by Malcolm's lawyer and I advised him I wished to comment on that decision, which had been based on what the board described as a lack of verifiable information about the boy seaman's presence during the war years aboard the vessels he named.

My comments begin with an excerpt from a letter of April 5, 1991, quoted in the appeal decision handed down by the British government's General Register and Record Office of Shipping and Seamen. That agency "failed to trace any reference to Mr. X in our Register of Seamen." It also states that there is no trace of the vessels *Willie S* or *Evelyn Evans* in their Register of Ships. These statements illustrate, I believe, that British records were flawed, to say the least. Apparently no attempt was made to pursue such information in Newfoundland government records, if such were in existence, as well as other sources in the island's archives. It seems to have been conveniently ignored by the research people, at least those in 1942, that Newfoundland was then ruled by the Commission of Government which had authority over the colony's affairs. It may be asked, for instance, were Newfoundland shipping records and port reports logged between the commission's takeover some years earlier and 1945 in custodial care in St. John's? It is apparent they were not forwarded to the British Record Office. There is no discernible evidence that such leads were pursued or their results, if any, are on record.

On May 10, 1991, the Newfoundland sub-regional director for Veterans Affairs states that his office carried out an extensive research program on merchant seamen and ships in Newfoundland. The result was a five-volume study, cross-referenced to names of ships they served on. The director advised that the appellant's name did not appear in any of the records. This elicits two observations: first, that vessels under fifty tons did not sail under articles; and second, if underaged boys were listed as crew members, that point may be considered relevant. My discussions with Newfoundland schooner men and those interested in the Atlantic region's marine history suggest that underaged boys were infrequently entered on crew lists, even if such lists were recorded and reported to shore authorities. There is reason to believe that deck and galley boys were supernumerary.

It is possible as well that there was some relation to civil authorities and their views on what effectively was child labour. Was there legislation relating to children working at sea and was the situation complicated by the divisive record-keeping structure within Newfoundland's divided school system in which four denominational groups operated the teaching process? It is possible, perhaps probable, that a poor boy could go aboard a vessel and sail on her for a couple of years without any questions being raised as long as the family did not object. For a young widow or for wives with children and husbands in poor health, there would be no objection. A few dollars could be sent home from the lad's pay to help out, money badly needed in a community suffering the pain and deprivation of the Depression.

The penultimate paragraph of the appeal board decision states: "There has been no evidence submitted from anyone who has sailed with the appellant on either of the two vessels." That statement exemplifies what may be described as a considerable gap in logic. Since it has already been established that no records exist (or had been found) of the applicant's name among the crew aboard either vessel in question, it could hardly be expected that statutory declarations could be obtained from putative shipmates of whom there is only distant recollection and absolutely no knowledge of where they might be. More than a half century has passed since Malcolm served aboard those vessels. A twenty-five or thirty-year-old shipmate of those times would be nearing eighty, if he were still alive. Seafaring was a difficult life: hard work and low pay, poor diet and medical negligence in the charity ward, if one was lucky enough to survive sickness or injury until the ship reached port.

There is growing conviction among merchant navy veterans that the so-called benefits that VAC now claims to be in effect represent only token recognition, based as they appear to be on the applicant's income being below the poverty line. The only fair acknowledgment of voluntary service in recognized theatres of war, which must include dangerous coastal waters as well as the high seas, would be a cash settlement. This would be practical recognition not only of cruelly belated acceptance as veterans, but also as appropriate recompense for vicious postwar discrimination, for years of exclusion from shore employment and educational programs. If the Canadian government can give financial compensation to Japanese-Canadians for their internment during the war, and to military veterans and prisoners-of-war, why are merchant navy veterans and prisoners-of-war refused compensation? Merchant marine veterans were interned at sea for all practical purposes.

Merchant seamen were effectively controlled; if they signed off a ship, they had about three weeks to sign on another vessel or report to a manning pool. After the end of hostilities, it was at least a year and a half later before they could legally apply for a shore job. Such employment was reserved for veterans of the Armed Forces, even those whose overseas service took place in the nine-mile ferry crossing between Cape Tormentine, New Brunswick and Borden, Prince Edward Island.

The reluctance to accept statutory statements from those who knew the applicants during the war and recalled the circumstances is inexcusable, legal perhaps, but inexcusable. There is, of course, the rarely used opportunity for ministerial discretion. The details are confidential. They refer to a service veteran's need for custodial health care, but minimal overseas service could not be verified. It was believed that he had crossed the Bay of Fundy by ferry between Digby and Saint John on an army posting during the war. That would have qualified him as an overseas veteran. A minister of veterans affairs interceded and the medical care was provided as a humanitarian measure. Justly so, yet was a double standard evident? It is unlikely that the same consideration would be extended to a wartime merchant mariner, considering the denial of veteran status by Veterans Affairs Canada for a half century.

Off the south coast of Cape Breton, Isle Madame is a picturesque place settled for more than two centuries. There, fishing and the sea are in the blood of families whose ancestors sailed westward from St. Malo, France to the rich fishing grounds off Acadia. Twenty-seven hundred nautical miles to the east in May 1945, the war in Europe officially ends and aboard the Canadian merchant ship *Champlain Park* proceeding northeast up the English Channel, is Francis Martell, a boy from Arichat on Isle Madame: "The water was filled with mines, but the anti-magnetic gear for kicking them away had been removed from the ship when the war ended. A lot of ships got blown out of the water. One ship at the dock exploded and burned right before my eyes. I was fifteen."

Francis had enlisted in the merchant marine at age fourteen; many of his friends did the same. "When I was thirteen, I played with Wilfred Samson in Petit de Grat. The next time I saw him was in Italy." Francis also speaks of a fourteen-year-old boy from Spryfield, now a part of Halifax, who was sent to the store by his mother to buy meat for supper. "He walked right past the store and down to the waterfront; he got a job that day aboard a Norwegian ship. Two days out of Halifax, the ship was torpedoed and he was taken aboard a German U-boat. Some time later he was transferred to a Japanese submarine and taken to Nagasaki where he was held in a prison camp until the war was over. When he arrived back home, it was the first anyone had heard from him since he left the house on the errand for his mother."

Francis says that for many young boys in a small community, joining the war effort was their only choice: "Things were terrible in 1944, it was the Depression and life wasn't easy. I had two brothers in the merchant marine. They would write and tell me about the places they had seen. I knew I could work, so I enlisted. It was great. Aboard ship there was lots to eat." In 1944 there was immediate need for crews for the Park ships, the government-owned fleet hastily put together in yards on both coasts and in the Great Lakes. Millions of tons of shipping had been lost in the first three years of the war and vessels were urgently needed to supply Allied armies and materials required by the war economy of Britain. The one hundred and seventy ships required more than six thousand men. Understandably, they signed on almost any healthy person available with little concern for age as long as the body was sturdy and the mind willing. The need for crews had led to establishment of merchant navy manning pools at Halifax, Saint John, Montreal, and Vancouver.

Francis observed that the merchant marine was made up of kids, older people and the handicapped, grinning at me as he spoke. I had been a classmate of his brother Bill Martell at radio school and he knew I had been a Category E Armed Forces reject who joined the merchant service. Francis used his brother's birth certificate to obtain a registration card; he didn't tell me if it was Bill's certificate or belonged to another brother. With the card he got a job as mess boy on a small vessel operating between ports on the Strait of Canso and Northumberland Strait. After a few weeks of sea time, Francis went to Halifax, reporting to the Shipping Office on Granville Street. There, he asked Mr. Preedy if there were any ship jobs.

Preedy looked over his spectacles: "How old are you lad?"

"Sixteen, sir."

"I wouldn't believe that at all. Hmmm." H.T. thumbed through his notebook. "Just happen to have a place aboard the *Clyde Valley*. Are you a good worker?"

"Yes, sir."

"All right then, lad. Be sure to write to your mum before you sail. She'll worry."

Francis joined the *Clyde Valley*, trading between the West Indies, Nova Scotia, and Newfoundland. Seeking distant places, he later joined the manning pool and shipped out on the *Champlain Park*, sailing the North Atlantic supply run. Because of the scarcity of Canadian merchant marine records — some destroyed by government decision after the war — many seaman had to search out their own proof of service. This was a common experience among those who sailed as boys. We cannot know how many now dead either knew or cared how to make such enquiries, and why bother if the government didn't seem to give a damn about merchant seamen. Francis Martell was one of the fortunate. He finally located his former captain in a North Sydney nursing home. The old skipper signed the statutory declaration that Francis had served on his ship beginning in 1943.

The reference to destruction of records could have two meanings. First, that those responsible for marine matters decided there was no point in sending documents to custodial care; they took up space in those pre-computer days and senior levels of government either were not aware that they existed or did not give a damn. Fragmentary records that have come to light reveal serious omissions. The second possibility is that local and regional records were probably disposed of to save space since there were no directives from Ottawa to retain them or ship them to the National Archives. The private records of shipping companies would have some information on personnel, but again, after a decade or two, the needs of posterity did not hold high priority, if considered at all.

In recent years, research relating to Canada's merchant marine during the war years has been conducted by Professor Foster Griezic at Carleton University, Ottawa. His work links events and policies of fifty years ago with the dismal response by a series of governments to merchant navy recognition. This curtain of neglect appears consistent with the pattern of intransigence and political expediency of the wartime government and subsequent administrations.

Politics pervades

With a tad more scandal and some observations on psychological stability, the history of Canadian governments between 1914 and 1945 would make an interesting work of fiction, challenging the imagination of readers. The towering political figure during most of these years was William Lyon Mackenzie King, whose physical presence was less than impressive and exemplified perhaps the median, a word the dictionary defines as "being in the middle or in an intermediate position." That could describe both his personal philosophy and his meditative thought processes: a decision delayed frequently reveals its own solution. His leadership during the latter years of the 1930s was less than outstanding, but the picture of King as wartime leader is an intriguing combination of muddling along, allowing events to proceed at their own pace, and the realpolitik of assessing all problems and challenges in direct relation to the Liberal Party and its continuance in power.

It may be difficult for a later generation to realize the impact and influence of political patronage and manipulation on public affairs and passive acceptance of such activities. Political management and manoeuvring in our time is somewhat less invidious, although there are times when it recalls memories of mid-century conditions in our land. What's good for the Liberal Party is what will keep it in power, a rule by which King lived until his final days. A case may be made that Liberal administrations were perhaps the right team to deal with problems of the time, operating from a middle-of-the-road position, halfway between the unhappy left, which included industrial workers as well as a substantial number of farmers and academics, and what would now be called the almost radical right held together by distrust of Liberals who were suspected of playing footsie with the socialists. Louis St. Laurent later described the CCF as "liberals in a hurry."

Students of political rhetoric may now suspect that current Liberal policies have slowed considerably and are progressing backward, particularly in social programs. Books in great number analyze government policies during the war years. They are valuable in giving us a wide assessment of how Canada responded to challenges at home and abroad. Yet remembrance of events seen firsthand draw a sharper picture than the learned interpretation of respected historians and research scholars. Mackenzie King's wartime leadership reflects the saying the man was right for the times, and it is perhaps unfair to criticize how he maintained national posture and purpose.

That being said, the use of patronage and preferment, instead of being placed on the back burner while we got on with the war, was applied down to the lowest level of bag-person and ward-heeler. The obvious exceptions involved necessity; war materials and supplies were needed urgently and an instant sellers market arose which included demand for items lying dormant in warehouses or back lots across the country. The slim inventories maintained in past months disappeared like snow in springtime, and calls went out for immediate increases in production within the capabilities of plants and personnel.

The hateful political weight of the backroom boys was nowhere more evident than in how you enlisted in the Armed Forces. I write about what I know from personal experience. In 1939, weeks after the declaration of war, I decided to enlist in the navy; I was raised by the sea and it was the natural thing to do. Many of my schoolmates served in the North Atlantic in the navy and the merchant marine. I reported to the recruiting office in HM Dockyard in Halifax and was given a pre-interview questioning by an NCO I thought was an old man, perhaps thirty-five or forty years of age. A pleasant chap, he said I would be interviewed by the recruiting officer. Even though no vacancies existed at the moment, that situation might change in coming months.

"Oh, do you have your letter with you?"

"Letter, sir. What letter?"

"Your letter from Gordon Isnor's office recommending you for enlistment if you are suitable." (Gordon B. Isnor was Member of Parliament for the constituency of Halifax.)

"I didn't know I needed one."

"Well, sorry, lad, but you do; they want to make sure that most new entries are from Grit families."

I left somewhat disappointed and a couple of weeks later was back with my letter. I was interviewed, given the M test, an intelligence test of sorts in which I had to say what was wrong with a table that had only three legs and other such matters. Manual dexterity and physical condition were assessed by an overweight naval reserve doctor wheezing as he worked and lighting one cigarette after another. I was rejected, category E, for defective eyesight. There had been a slim chance the decision would be reconsidered, but the navy decided it had no provision for the visually handicapped who would never be allowed to go to sea. That interview came to mind in later years as I clung to a wing of the bridge with one hand and worked the Aldis lamp with the other. My visual defect had one advantage, my eyes were unusually sensitive to glare and I could see through fog, almost.

The next stop on my search for the King's shilling was the army, an anti-aircraft unit, where applicants were scarce and a letter of recommendation from a political dignitary was unnecessary. I had kept the original letter from the MP's office in case it was needed. The army did things differently. They tested me in typing, shorthand and filing and, the ever-present M test, before sending me to the medical folks. There, a young corporal gave me the eye test and tried hard to bend the rules, but the medical officer interceded, expressing regrets. In later weeks, I undertook two failed attempts to enlist in the air force, but they too were dubious about a cousin weakeyes in the service. With that I entered radio school to qualify for service at sea, to sail under the old Red Duster worn by British merchant vessels.

Another example of political influence in smoothing the path for potential recruits occurred a year later when two young men from a family I knew wished to join the RCAF. They went to a small business person with an office on Granville Street in Halifax, a political bagman I am told whose recommendation carried unwritten, but none the less effective, authority. Again, only if the candidate passed the physical examination. A political recommendation wasn't required when I was recalled for army examination in 1944. They were scraping the bottom of the barrel, while the fat apples sheltered in the ranks of the zombies. My eyesight test was now acceptable for home service and since the M test marks were high, I was slung over to the resident shrink, a medical officer with some training in psychiatry. This was done on the reasonable assumption that if an applicant was too smart, he could be a nut or a trouble-maker. I told the chap the reason for my remarkably correct answers to the questionnaire: I'd taken it four times before.

"Well, you've passed the physical. They have lower standards now and you may be recommended for officer training. You're a high school drop-out according to your records, but then some of our best officers are."

"Well, I'm an officer now with considerable time in the North Atlantic theatre, and I'm too young for the veterans guard. I guess it's back to sea."

The captain looked up, "I don't think so, unless you apply for exemption. As it stands now, you'll be asked to report on Monday morning."

It was probably inevitable, but I didn't like the idea of being a file clerk on home service; who in hell would know you weren't a zombie. I went back to the ship and reported to the Old Man.

"Like hell you will. On Monday we'll be at sea and I do not accept anyone's authority to take one of my crew. Now go and have a double rum while I use the telephone."

I went back to my cabin and poured a slug of rum then sat down in my only chair that took up a third of my floor space. So, what would be the alternative if the Old Man couldn't persuade Ottawa to make an exception, a rather remote possibility considering his modest level of diplomacy; it would be an adversarial conversation. In traditional Nova Scotian style, I thought of the last resort in emergencies, an appeal to my Member of Parliament; his recommendation had been part of the enlistment process in previous years. MPs had enormous influence, sitting at the right hand of God or his henchman, Mackenzie King.

I was just pouring a second rum when the quartermaster knocked on my door: "Captain's compliments, sir. He wants to see you." I slugged down half the drink and went out on deck and forward. The Old Man was at his desk and waved me to sit down.

"I couldn't get through to the director of merchant shipping, but his assistant said he will deal with it and Arthur Randles himself will call the Department of National Defence and tell them again to keep their hooks off Canadians serving in the merchant marine. I also advised his second in command that because we are UK registry, our crews are not subject to external authority. I am advising you not to apply for exemption or report to the army."

It was either good advice or everything fell into place; the army was not heard from again, ever, but we wouldn't know what had happened for three months. On return to home port, the captain was told that deferment was granted until the draftee was further advised. We had sailed for the Gulf of Mexico on Saturday. My absence would have been reported when I failed to show up at Military District 6 on Monday morning, unless MD6 in Halifax had been advised that Fraser, W.D. had been granted deferment. If not, the RCMP would be advised that the man in question was adrift or whatever term they wished to use. If I had been called up for home service only because of medical category, would I have borne the lifelong stigma of being a "zombie" and devoid of an opportunity to vote myself out of the war, as had six hundred men aboard *HMCS Uganda* in the Pacific?

The ears of youth record well and accurately when exposed innocently to the realities of observed practice: a society in which political parties in power had something very close to absolute authority over so many aspects of life, road work, government jobs, appointments from pound-keeper to overseer of the poor; government influence infernal. Its tentacles, working through local or district committees, affected general employment opportunity to the point where private companies followed a party hiring list when jobs opened. If firms didn't cooperate, difficulty might arise in winning tenders for government services or supplies. It is a disturbing thought to consider that in the 1930s we Canadians lived in a country established on religious and democratic principles but one in which patronage and nepotism were the new religion or rather a continuance of the Family Compact principle and remnants of the European class system. We were taking some tentative steps toward a kinder, gentler society, as long as the reality of political power was sustained and refined.

It calls for the skill and scholarship of a thoroughly perceptive historian to comprehend a national leader's mind-set when it is as complicated and deliberate as that of Mackenzie King. He was a link between the Victorian age and our century of wars, revolutions, and social upheaval. So busy with political manoeuvring and following his own star in various directions, including toward the heavens, this man of advanced education seems in retrospect almost fatally unaware of the reality of international political events. It was a time when any English-speaking person above the age of fifteen realized fascism was a menace rather than a welcome return to absolute authority. Mackenzie King considered himself the ultimate Liberal; inside his head he retained the small-c, yet none the less influential, narrow focus of the conservative Presbyterian. Authority from the pulpit or the throne was the source of spiritual and social order.

Social order involved control of policies and events, if possible and perhaps at almost any cost, that reflected his wishes and inclinations. They blinded him perhaps to the obvious stupidity, if not irresponsibility, of pursuing the idea of visiting Adolph Hitler as a side trip from King's visit to the Imperial Conference in London during May and June 1937. The visit had been opposed a year earlier by the Under-secretary of State, O.D. Skelton, apparently because as something of an isolationist, Skelton thought it demeaning or at least inappropriate. He was one of many senior bureaucrats and advisers with somewhat less than a comprehensive perception of international affairs and suspicion of other countries and ethnic groups. Something of this attitude of ignorance, bigotry, and anti-semitism was behind the heartless wave-off of a shipload of refugees from Canadian shores (as had been done by the United States), condemning them to a return voyage to Europe and the death camps. The removal and internment of Japanese citizens of Canada was another example not only of war-induced panic but an extension of the "yellow peril" fanaticism of the 1930s on the west coast of Canada and the United States. In the U.S. it is now the "Latin peril" as Spanish-speaking agricultural and service labourers seek citizenship status and education for their children.

In his diary impressions of the meeting with Hitler, King noted that the dictator was a religious man of humble origin, a teetotaller, vegetarian, abstemious, and unmarried. Except for King's enjoyment of a good wine, these qualities mirrored his own characteristics, surely a complimentary comparison. Prime Minister King wrote that a person of such values "could not be other than eminently wise." He joined the immortals of understatement with the further observation that Hitler's "dictatorship is a means to an end, needed perhaps to make the Germans conscious of themselves." Secret musings of a prime minister of Canada, his mind in a dream world and his heart among the spirits.

Two years after the conversation in Berlin, we were at war with Nazi Germany. Britain declared war on September 3, 1939, and Canada joined the conflict seven days later, a week in which King's crystal ball got a serious working over. A prelude to war, six years of sacrifice and toil at home and the physical and spiritual wounds of the battlefield, the oceans, and hostile skies.

Fort Astoria (SS Yarmouth County)
West Coast Shipbuilders constructed the 10,000 ton *Fort Astoria* at their Vancouver yard. Owned by Acadia Overseas Freighters Ltd. she was put into service in 1943 and became the *Yarmouth County* in 1946. (Photo W. Simpson Collection, Maritime Museum of the Atlantic, N18629)

Pay and income tax

A decades-old erroneous assumption, if not deliberately self-serving on the part of governments and veterans associations, is that merchant seamen were paid more than service people. This is obvious in the correspondence and comments of those who ought to know better or take the trouble to investigate the facts. A couple of generations have been exposed to the detestable opinions heard to this day fifty years later from too many bureaucrats, journalists, and most regrettably young reporters. One of them asked me during our Halifax demonstration in August 1995, if it was true most merchant mariners went to sea to get high pay and stay out of the army. When I told her the truth, that our pay was lower than service pay for equivalent rank and our benefits were non-existent, she looked incredulous.

"I tried to enlist four times but was found medically unfit; not a few of those who were aboard merchant ships were rejected by the Armed Forces. Some others went to sea at fourteen, fifteen, or sixteen years of age but were able to serve as deck or galley boys. You should know that the Second World War was a war of principle against fascism and genocide, something ordinary people sensed well ahead of our so-called political leaders. To unemployed lads it was the opportunity for a job."

The reporter checked her notebook: "But the Veterans Affairs people told me an hour ago that merchant marine pay was higher than that paid in the Armed Forces and that you are now eligible for equal benefits."

My response was courteous but blunt: "A trained reporter does not depend on hearsay without checking the facts. Did you study Canadian history in high school or university?" There was no response. Reporters ask questions but don't have time for a dialogue.

Little wonder that false impressions began and continued through the years. Government correspondence maintained that merchant seamen were paid more than those in the services. The final report of the Interdepartmental Committee on Merchant Seaman (1946) stated: "The comparison between the pay of a single merchant seaman and a single private soldier shows the serviceman at a considerable disadvantage." It certainly would, considering that the comparison is loaded with inaccuracies from the start. First, there was no difference in pay between a single and married merchant seaman. Family considerations were not and never have been a factor in the pay of a civilian mariner. The individual was paid for his work and qualifications for the task. An able-seaman had qualified through experience, first as a boy seaman, then ordinary seaman, then able-bodied seaman. There are other inconsistencies I will note later.

Deck and engineer officers as well as radio officers were and are qualified by a certificate issued by federal shipping authorities following written examinations. A so-called "ticket" is solid evidence of ability and commitment, and with infrequent exceptions is the proof of years of sea time and experience, a very considerable disparity in relation to the training and experience of a new-entry soldier or naval rating. Only in the later years of the war did merchant ships accept people with minimal experience. The interdepartmental committee report bases its assumption on an erroneous juxtaposition of pay rates. It compares the 1940 rates for service people and the 1944 rates for merchant mariners. Further, the figures do not include the supply of uniforms, medical attention and health care, allowances for wife and/or children, and the ubiquitous income tax that applied to civilian mariners but not to service people with a minimum of two weeks at sea during a six-month period. If a merchant mariner lost his life other than by enemy action, such as a collision between ships in a convoy or elsewhere, his wife and children received no compensation.

There is also the matter of the so-called war bonus for merchant mariners. That bonus in addition to the estimated cost of so-called postwar benefits totalled an average of $339.70 per seamen for the duration. An additional $212.19 was paid to those having service prior to April 1, 1944, bringing the overall average to $551.81. Cash received was on average less because that total included the nebulous postwar benefits. The base pay of merchant seamen was subject to income tax, but they would not receive either base pay or bonus unless they were on ship's articles. That situation did not change until the merchant seamen manning pools were formed in 1941. Those who joined were entitled to base pay only while awaiting assignment. The war-bonus/danger-pay was only payable when the individual joined a ship. The merchant navy bonus was twenty-five per cent for those sailing in dangerous waters with ten per cent additional for tankers. A further ten per cent was added, payable only to members of the manning pool. It is interesting to note that another discriminatory requirement appeared in the regulations. The manning pool could require a seaman to join an Allied vessel for which bonuses were not payable, such as a ship under the Polish flag or sign aboard a Greek vessel believed to be unseaworthy, not an uncommon condition among vessels of certain occupied countries and some of our own.

Federal authorities' attitudes toward merchant navy prisoners-of-war are less than consistent with Armed Forces POWs. A prime example is the fact that merchant seamen prisoners had their wages frozen at the time of capture. I met a former ship's cook who was captured off France in 1940 and held prisoner for five years. On his release, he was given five years base pay of approximately $5,000, minus $1,800 income tax. He was unwell for some years after the war, but medical treatment was not available except in the charity ward. The sick mariners arrangement had little if anything to offer toward treatment of chronic illness even though the medical problem was attributed to prison camp conditions.

In the examination of pay comparisons between the merchant marine and the Armed Forces, it may be noted that an allowance for an average family consisting of a wife and two children is not included in the naval pay rates. There were no family allowances for a merchant mariner be he a captain or ordinary seaman. The monthly rates may then be compared.

For those of a later generation relying only on hearsay or lacking comprehension of general wage levels, it may be useful to offer some general observations on social and economic conditions a half century ago. It was a time when union representation was largely confined to major industrial operations. Regardless of such exceptions, wages were low, and again with even fewer exceptions, did not keep up with the rise in consumer prices caused by diminishing production as factories turned to war support materials. By way of comparison, the purchasing power of a dollar then would be the equivalent of about twenty dollars in current purchasing power. A dollar was a big piece of our pay in the late 1930s, particularly in rural areas, if we were lucky enough to be employed. By contrast, income of $200 a week in our times is far below the poverty line. In the 1930s and early '40s wages were barely above the subsistence level.

In the following table, note that in most cases, masters of merchant ships were paid by mutual agreement with the owners. Consequently, figures are not generally available. From the few figures on record, the rates for master are about five per cent above those for a chief engineer. All figures for the merchant marine include base pay, war bonus, and a ten per cent bonus for tanker service or membership in a manning pool. Again, bonuses did not apply until a merchant seaman signed on a ship.

Average monthly pay rates in 1940:

RC Navy	Merchant Navy	RCN	Merchantman
Cmdr.	Chief Engineer	$382	$345
L/Cdr.	Chief Officer	$363	$225
L/Cdr.	2nd Engineer	$363	$225
Lt.	2nd Mate	$312	$200
Lt.	3d Engineer	$289	$206
Sub/Lt.	Chief Radio Officer	$232	$165
Sub/Lt.	(Radio, Mate, Eng)	$232	$155
Bos'n	L/Seaman	$142.50	$110
Able Seaman		$133.50	$86
Ordinary Seaman		$123	$55
Stoker/Fireman		$137	$89

In 1940, pay for all merchant navy ratings was much lower than that for Royal Canadian Navy ratings at the same level. That continued until 1944 when pay increased. No merchant marine officer under the rank of captain or chief engineer received as much pay as the RCN equivalent, even in 1944.

The treatment of POWs after escape or release in Europe was a disgrace, no less accusative word exists. The following comparisons illustrate the gratuitous anomaly of the wartime administration and succeeding governments.

POW Postwar Benefits	Military POW	MN POW
Clothing allowance	$100	None
Rehabilitation grant	Yes	None
Medical & dental care	1 year	Only if disabled
University training	Yes	None
Civil service preference	Yes	None
Business & professional loans	Yes	None
Service time, sea capture	Open-ended	Prison gate
Service time, land capture	Open-ended	No MN POW time

This is a partial list. When benefits are indicated, they are almost beyond reach because of the dispute over records with the onus of proof placed on the applicant. And the longer a POW was interned, the lower the average rate of payment per month in custody. The rate is beneficially slanted in favour of military POWs.

At the end of the war, merchant navy pay was somewhat better but not as high as naval pay levels for equivalent ranks. A cause of further worry involved the already apparent efforts of the Canadian government to sell off much if not most of its merchant marine. In protest against the gutting of the fleet as a matter of government policy, merchant navy people demonstrated in September 1945 below the Peace Tower, a singular monument to their impending unemployment. The local and national press recorded the event and noted it was supported by boards of trade, chambers of commerce, Eatons and even the *Globe and Mail*, a publication regarded as the reactionary voice of Upper Canada and barely visible in its concern for working people. The Canadian Maritime Commission of the time went through the motions and tried to make a case for moving the merchant marine into the Royal Canadian Navy, a marriage of convenience and a rather stupid proposal at a time when the navy itself was facing major reductions in budget, personnel, and ships. The maritime commission's report was ignored down to the last comma and the document joined dusty files on a quiet shelf in the archives, the final resting place of long-ignored and finally forgotten paperwork.

At that time, during the immediate postwar months, regulations still prevented seamen from leaving Canada to ship aboard a foreign vessel, even though the chance of a berth in Canada had all but disappeared. That policy of continued refusal to allow us to seek work on foreign ships at a time when our own fleet was being sold, laid up, or scrapped and those afloat sailed under foreign flags, amounts to little less than internment. It was a dismal combination of conditions: unemployed with no postwar benefits or training. All available jobs ashore were kept beyond reach on the other side of the invisible fence that separated merchant marine veterans from the employment and educational opportunities provided demobilized Armed Forces personnel.

Fifty years in limbo has been the fate of Canadian seaman. Governments either refused recognition of merchant mariners' wartime effort or have offered only empty-pocket lip-service to the principle of equality with others whose wartime service, while commendable, was not measurably greater. Neither governments nor shipping interests were much concerned about mariner's pay rates during the war years. After the war, governments bowed out of such considerations and shipping firms returned to their former unregulated practices.

Repressive policies are still with us and notably aboard the shadowy flag-of-convenience vessels registered in Panama, Liberia, Liechtenstein, etc. Their officers are of varied competence and their crews scraped up at bargain pay in the Philippines, the Middle East, and other sources of half-starved labour, manpower not available during the war. The innate hypocrisy of government may be measured by the fact that while they realized shipboard job prospects were dim and getting dimmer, marine technical courses would be provided for merchant seamen. This at a time when direct and deliberate moves were afoot to sell most of the Park fleet without plans for replacement with new and better ships. Of course, Ottawa was aware that seamen's unions were sniffing at the opportunity to sign up members and negotiate contracts. As well, more than a suspicion held that union organizers were communists or at least socialists. That red cloud on the postwar horizon caused shivers up the comfortable spines along the Rideau River. The government exercised the tempting option of importing a gangster to take control of our seamen's union. It didn't matter much; in a short time there would be no ships and no crews to pay dues.

There has been more than enough gratuitous misinformation on matters that are now history and with appropriate records to refute the generalities and obfuscations. Time is growing short for surviving merchant mariners of the Second World War to wash the mud from page after page of innuendo and accusation.

John Masefield described it best:

> Man with his burning soul
> Has but an hour of breath
> To build a ship of Truth.

The Foundation Security
The deepwater salvage tug *Founation Security* is shown at her pier in Halifax, Nova Scotia, in the 1940s. Owned by Foundation Maritime Ltd., she operated in the waters of the northwest Atlantic. She and her sister ship, *Foundatin Franklin*, and other craft owned by the company played a major role in salvage operations off Canada's Atlantic coast before, during and after the war years. (Photo Maritime Museum of the Atlantic N-17071)

Postwar pariahs

After the years of war in which many of our number were lost at sea, and not a few of them became hypothetical casualties, survivors faced the outbreak of peace and the infinitely less dangerous challenge of life ashore. For the vast majority of civilian seamen, as we were frequently described, a shore job was the immediate goal; we knew it would be difficult to find one for various reasons. The postwar economy would have to be geared up to take advantage of markets everyone hoped would be available. People believed there would be swift growth in demand for consumer goods either not produced for six years or largely allocated to the war effort.

To encourage and sustain manufacturing in the country's principal industrial centres, there arose an obvious need for jobs and for a workforce with enough money in the pay packet to allow for some discretionary spending for stoves, refrigerators, and other consumer items to be bought mostly on what the English euphemistically refer to as hire purchase.

It is difficult for children and grandchildren to understand the economic conditions of a postwar nation which moved rather precipitously from the Hungry Thirties to a war footing, when money that could not be raised over a decade of depression to stimulate business and employment was borrowed miraculously to help pay for the fight against fascism. It was indeed a noble cause, yet we lived in a country like many others in which relative stages of poverty among many was considered the norm and beyond human ingenuity to correct. Those who questioned the lack of incentive to improve social conditions were largely considered radical, if not revolutionary.

Canada's surviving merchant fleet had already begun its rapid postwar decline. The majority of vessels were Park ships, hastily built in established or quickly organized yards on both coasts, the St. Lawrence River, and the Great Lakes. Other ships included tankers carrying petroleum from the Caribbean fields to refineries in Montreal and Dartmouth, and some smaller ships delivering oil to regional locations. A return to the insular attitudes of the 1920s and '30s, during which the federal government damned merchant shipping with faint praise, was evident after 1945 when those who served in the fleet were praised with faint damns, occasional kind words, and benevolent neglect. With his ship tied up at the pier and the crew signed off, Able Seaman Jones went ashore with his suitcase, pay, and his discharge paper, a document that carried the large letters VG (Very Good) which indicated he could be signed on again when needed. The initials DC (Decline to Report) had an ominous meaning: troublemaker or perhaps lazy. In Canada, an unfavourable discharge could be torn up and, if questioned, the gap in service time could be ascribed to sick-leave or necessary work on the home farm. In the United Kingdom, the practice was to use a discharge book in which the numbered page carrying a DC report could not be removed unnoticed. That condition pretty well ensured that sea-lawyers or layabouts were weeded out early.

The unemployed seaman could go to his home for a couple of weeks and after a series of good meals and clothes washed he would head back to a city or town to see what jobs were open to a willing worker. And that is where the stonewalls loomed. The merchant navy didn't mean much, if anything, to people who lived in communities not associated with the sea. Citizens related life on the ocean to those who wore a naval uniform and, particularly as you moved inland, you came to the conclusion that a majority of Canadians were unaware of the existence of ships that did not have guns or fight great battles for the Empire.

Choices were few and in most cases hardly existent. With only rare exceptions, we could neither apply for nor be interviewed for vacancies in the federal civil service. Personnel people asked the job applicant if he was a veteran. Some of them, good hearts indeed, wrote down yes after they were told no, but in the merchant marine. Those worthies, who deserve warm memories, were disobeying direct instructions from supervisors who observed government policy. Unfortunately, their kind efforts were in vain, the application form required specifics of military service and the name of units.

In general, the private sector was just as negative. An individual looking for work in the retail trade or on construction jobs encountered the obvious preference for ex-service people. This was particularly patronizing when the person doing the hiring was ex-service. As late as the 1980s, the Corps of Commissionaires did not accept merchant navy veterans. A personnel man whose brother was lost in a U-boat attack got into difficulties with his superiors when he objected to the bias against merchant veterans. His boss advised him that he had to follow federal regulations. It did not take many weeks of job-seeking to realize that something was very wrong. Jobs were opening in various sectors as evidence of growing confidence that the economy would expand instead of shrink back into postwar recession, but they were not open to us.

Opportunities for subsidized training or education at any level were also closed to merchant navy applicants. Many of our group had sailed pre-war and were now middle-aged after going to sea barely out of their teens, not equipped to surmount unfavourable prospects.

In retrospect, it appears there can be more than a suspicion that a social division existed between common seaman and other sectors of society; if in uniform, an individual's lack of social graces or adequate vocabulary could be excused, if not condoned. The wartime merchant seaman, ashore in civilian clothes, might be thought an avoider of military service or medically unfit. That impression was communicated rather more often than not, particularly when we were away from coastal communities. I shudder to think of the attitudes of some prairie people for instance. In later years many of them responded with a blank stare when they asked if I had been in the navy and I said no. They did not pursue the matter and I had no wish to confuse them further with the observation that oceans of the world were not the unquestioned realm of bluejackets. Either history was not well taught or was not high on the list of mandatory subjects.

In the immediate postwar years, it was supremely evident that if a job-seeker was not a former service person, there were two strikes against him. I use the pronoun him for the very good reason that in those semi-enlightened days, women were suffering traditional discrimination that exists to this day and hour. A goodly percentage of them are working today for lower pay than males in the same classification. As Casey Stengel said: "You could look it up." My own experience in job hunting was an exception, an accident resulting from a lucky coincidence. I applied for a technical job with the Canadian Broadcasting Corporation in Halifax, either as a studio operator there or transmitter technician at Sackville, New Brunswick, site of the CBC International Service transmitters.

The CBC's regional engineer, Maurice (Moe) Smith, was stationed at the Sackville installation and visited Halifax on a regular basis to oversee technical operations. As he began my interview I wondered what this tall acerbic man was really like. I soon found out; courteous and precise and with a less than enthusiastic opinion of program people, announcers and producers. Moe scanned my application form and the test results for manual dexterity, circuitry, and general broadcasting theory. Basic stuff and yet simple enough for we of little experience to provide some indication that we were at a modest level of skills. If hired, that would be confirmed by regular and careful review of our progress.

"Hmmm, not bad, a little rusty maybe. And you've been a marine radio operator for a few years?"

"Yes, sir, an endorsed second-class licence, never had enough shore time to write the first-class exam."

"Well, goddamit, you needn't bother now. I worked my way through college as a sparks on the Great Lakes and I'm always ready to recommend a brother of the cloth as the old man used to say." I think the engineer's dad was a clergyman, Moe certainly had absorbed a biblical vocabulary at some stage of his career. He closed the application file and initialled it.

"You're hired. When can you start?"

"In two weeks time, sir."

"Okay, report to Arleigh Canning on the way out. He'll confirm the starting date. Oh yes, you'll be described as a temporary employee for awhile, but the job can be confirmed a bit later. In the meantime, there won't be any nosy questions about whether the new guy was in the Armed Forces. I don't want any personnel clerk interfering in my choice of technical people. Now, for God's sake call me Moe, I haven't been ordained yet and not likely to be." With that Moe raised his six-foot-two frame from the chair and squeezed my hand so tightly his engineer's iron ring dented my fingers painfully.

Arleigh Canning was the technical director of the Halifax operation and had given me the initial tests. When I entered his office, he looked up.

"I thought you'd be back. Moe liked the tests, but I think he liked your marine experience even more. It used to be his trade too. Anyway, sit down and I'll get the training schedule lined up. I'll schedule you for Monday, the eleventh, if that's okay."

"Yes, I'll sign-off when I get back aboard."

Arleigh began his pencil work and I waited, looking at the sign pinned to his desk light. It was precise, terse even: "Don't go away mad, just go away!" I soon learned that it was his usual response to producers who called in looking for one of our few good microphones for their show. Most of our mikes and remote amplifiers had been royal visit specials from the King and Queen's visit to Canada in 1939; they would continue to be used for years and finally put out to pasture as sound-effects pickups.

I returned to the ship and reported to the master; he took the news without any great expression of regret, although I had hoped he would wish me well. He did, in the form of a challenge.

"Well now, a new career beckons; makes me think of the times I changed jobs, half apprehensive at the prospect of new responsibilities and glad to get away from the evil influences of your shipmates. I hope you'll think of us kindly in future days." With that, Captain Adamson offered the closest evidence of a friendly smile I had observed on his generously plump features over several years.

"Now, one task before you pack up. I wish to provide you with a suitable recommendation. You will write it for me in the next day or two and the exercise will be useful practice in diplomacy."

"Yes, sir, and thank you."

One didn't ask him how to do something; once ordered it was the recommended course to proceed to the task. The captain nodded and walked through the curtain into his day cabin. As I slid the typewriter out on its shelf bolted to the desk, I heard the sound of ice cubes and a liquid being poured. Just as I complained silently that he should have offered me a farewell drink, his voice boomed out: "Come in, young man, and we'll have a double dram of Bowmore." It was expensive and it was "unco guid," as befitted a single malt. I still have a copy of that letter which may possibly have been a forerunner of future events. It is couched in diplomatic terms, positive yet without expressed responsibility should a potential referee grouse that the individual's skills, deportment, or level of qualification were exaggerated.

When read through decades later, the letter stood up well as a model for thousands of letters I would write for political people in one of my subsequent reincarnations.

"Hmmmn," The Old Man read it, then read it again. "Suitable to the occasion, as brief and non-committal as a Highlander's confession." He signed it with a flourish, W. Adamson, Master, CS Cyrus Field.

"Thank you, sir."

"And thank you, it's been some good years, eh. And come back to visit from time to time. Good luck, and now you can call me Bill."

I was already packed and I walked back aft through the narrow passage between the lifeboats and the engineroom grating to the comfortable sixty square feet of my cabin. I left a few technical books for whomever would succeed me, took a last look around and with burberry and suitcase proceeded back toward the gangway and off the old tub.

I was ready for new responsibilities but nervous too; after years of familiar duties, a comfortable bunk and food and booze in abundance, if modest in quality, shore employment would be a momentous change. For we lucky few, employment on shore was the opportunity of a lifetime to avoid being beached without trades or any type of experience useful to industry. Eighteen months after the end of hostilities, it was more than evident that federal authorities had no interest in refining and developing a Canadian merchant fleet. If one was to exist in future years, it would be launched by the private sector. The oil companies would maintain their fleet of carriers serving South American fields for Canadian refineries, and ensure that their anti-union bias would continue. With fewer and fewer ships available, it was a buyer's market for shipping firms and people were the commodity. An engineer I know went for an interview and when he arrived at the top of the gangway, the chief engineer met him face to face and asked him if he was for or against unions. The response with expletives avoided was brief and the meeting ended abruptly with a less than polite farewell to the interviewer.

Other than the oil companies, where vacancies were filled by benevolent nepotism with an occasional exception, shipping berths were almost non-existent. Canadian merchant service people were signed off articles and dropped ashore without hope or prospects. The technical skills of engineers offered some advantage in job-seeking, and radio operators might be hired in communications trades. For able bodied seamen and deck officers, berths ashore proved rare indeed, although a few of the fo'c'sle hands were taken on by construction and engineering firms. The great mass of sea-going people no longer needed in what Canada saw as its continental future was a sad commentary on the lack of perception or foresight on the part of a government whose vision blanked out abruptly beyond the three-mile limit. Had any effort been made to plan for the future of more than twelve thousand men and several hundred women effectively demobilized from a vital segment of the war effort.

The answer is an emphatic no! A blatant evasion of responsibility is the kindest term one can apply to the government of Canada. The fault should be shared among prime ministers, their cabinets, and their advisers among whom could not be found a corporal's guard of people with knowledge of shipping either in peace or in wartime. If experienced people were actually available in government service, they were below the levels of influence. It is also possible that they offered advice which was filed away misunderstood or unread. Was the matter subject to consultation or already cast in concrete by the federal cabinet's presumptive post-war policies?

Autumn 1945. The Second World War ends with victory in Europe and in the Far East. Now begins the long years of occupation and emergency programs to help feed and clothe millions of refugees and ongoing attempts to sort out hordes of emaciated survivors released from concentration camps. Europe is awash in a tide of human beings in various stages of distress or facing imminent starvation. The resurgence of the temporarily dormant and mutual distrust between the West and the Soviet Union evident at the Yalta conference added dangerous complications to the rebirth of an economy needed to feed the vast population from the steppes to the Irish Sea.

We read much about stateless persons. In retrospect it seems that veterans of the merchant marine suffered less severe but obviously demeaning handicaps to employment, education, medical benefits, and a standard of living near the poverty line. Our memories were still vivid of the callous treatment of the unemployed in the Hungry Thirties, infamous work camps, and the denunciation of labour unions as communist-inspired. The military war might have been over, but the class war rolled right along, fuelled by an unhealthy fixation with what the so-called establishment perceived as the guilt, the dishonesty, and the lack of ambition of working people. The golden opinion that human laziness is responsible for unemployment remained enshrined in the affluent livingrooms of comfortable suburbs in our major cities. It surfaces occasionally in our own times. The same old slogans are polished up and trotted out for the approval of such think tanks as the Fraser Institute. (No relation.)

For eighteen months during the postwar period, we of the new underclass were precluded from employment opportunities ashore because we were not considered veterans of the Armed Forces. There were no rehabilitation programs, no clothing allowance — although a so-called war bonus was hardly more than enough to buy an economy suit and a pair of shoes. And for the person signed off a ship and with no prospects of another berth at sea, there wasn't even the courtesy of a medical or dental examination. Furthermore, the Canadian government gave no indication specific or implied that it wished to hear from us again. In later years, we would hear rumours that modest pensions might be available to merchant navy seamen able to prove their disease or disability resulted from enemy action on the high seas. If your infirmity, however, was caused by accident or the result of your ship being torpedoed within North American coastal waters, no pension applied.

It was and has always been heartless discrimination against thousands of volunteers unrecognized for loyal service to their King, a calculated effort to demean by unfair accusation, force-fed prejudice, and the nurturing of a tissue of lies such as "You fellows don't have any records." Perhaps the most damming aspect of five decades of calculated neglect is that merchant navy veterans are absent from any list of government advisers or consultants. In fact, the dice are loaded against our position because the federal government listens to everyone else in their so-called Consultative Group.

As recently as June 1996, it was déjà vu all over again; Canadian newspapers carried reports that the minister of national defence had paid $100,000 to a former campaign worker and member of the Greco-Canadian community to explain to that group why the government had discontinued benefits to veterans of the anti-Nazi underground in other countries. Thirty million dollars in benefits had been paid out before the federal government stopped the program in 1995; payments began in 1985 and most recipients were Canadian citizens who had emigrated from Greece.

On July 28, 1996, CTV carried an item on its network late news. It reported that RCMP information about a highly sensitive police investigation into claims made under the benefits program had been passed on by the office of the minister of national defence to senior officials in the Department of Veterans Affairs. It was alleged that the benefits cost taxpayers millions of dollars in claims. The CTV reporter claimed that a former campaign worker requested confidential information on the RCMP investigation. CTV News said it had obtained documents that showed the RCMP provided details about their sensitive investigation to senior bureaucrats in the department of national defence. Classified documents reveal that the former campaign worker asked senior veterans affairs or defence officials about the status of the RCMP investigation. He was told it would be inappropriate for him to approach the RCMP for information about their criminal investigation. The CTV report also said that a senior bureaucrat advised the person there was no need to contact the RCMP because they kept in touch, regularly informing the department about important developments in the high-profile investigation. The official was quoted as saying the arrangement worked well because it conveniently avoided any perception that the minister would be seen as interfering with the police investigation. The senior RCMP investigator confirmed that information was being passed on to senior government officials.

Except for a few in the inner circle of government, Canadians knew little, if anything, about the $30 million doled out to the former partisans. Few people would begrudge veterans benefits to individuals verified as members of the anti-Nazi underground in the occupied countries. It may be asked if a comparable effort was undertaken to ensure merchant marine veterans received deserved benefits.

Over a stretch of years, misleading if not false statements have been issued by a parade of federal cabinet ministers responsible for veterans affairs. It continues. We make our own judgments on whether these policy statements that merchant navy veterans are entitled to the same benefits as Armed Forces veterans are petrified truth. Either they represent the ministers' sincere beliefs (although some have recently recanted) or they continue to reflect the attitudes of some of their advisers, including former senior officers of the Armed Forces.

In 1992, then Veterans Affairs Minister Gerald Merrithew admitted that seamen were purposely excluded from being designated "war" veterans. That is consistent with our deliberate exclusion from the War Veterans Allowance Act. The truth is that merchant marine veterans come under acts of parliament that relate to civilian war veterans such as auxiliary services, firemen, etc., all groups deserving of full consideration having risked their lives in an active war zone. It may be recalled as well that immediate postwar regulations on restoration in civil employment, civil service employment preference, etc., all avoided recognition that merchant seamen ever existed. The emphasis was and has been on Armed Forces veterans whether they had served overseas or not. There are some alive who would make a virtue of necessity; there are others who make a convenience of hypocrisy.

The Lady Rodney on the St. Lawrence River at Quebec City
The *Lady Rodney*, along with her sister ship the *Lady Nelson*, was one of two Lady ships belonging to Canadian National Steamship Line which survived the war. During the war, she often carried Canadian soldiers to Europe. After the war the *Lady Rodney* brought hundreds of "war brides" to Canada — British, Dutch and other European women who married those Canadian servicemen. The other three Lady ships, the *Lady Hawkins*, *Lady Somers*, and *Lady Drake*, were war casualties. The Maritime Museum of the Atlantic on Lower Water Street, Halifax is home to a huge model of the *Lady Rodney*. (Photo: Maritime Museum of the Atlantic, M79.152.1

The last hurrah

On the warmest day in several decades throughout much of Canada, August 9, 1995, a pitifully small number of merchant marine veterans demonstrated across the country. In Ottawa, in provincial capitals and major cities aging survivors of the twelve thousand merchant seamen who served during the Second World War demonstrated in front of the buildings wherein Veterans Affairs Canada maintains its offices.

Few indeed! On that day the number of survivors of the cohorts who served on civilian ships during the 1939-45 conflict was estimated at 3,050, the average age being seventy-eight. A majority are in various stages of infirmity. Many are widowers living in modest circumstances with only a few fading pictures left in their package of small remembrances of a time long ago when they were young and strong. Do any of them deserve the decades of neglect, the absence of appropriate recognition, the complete vacuum of educational and health benefits with some very recent and very minor exceptions?

When we began to organize a symbolic demonstration across the country, our comrades found that many people they asked to participate were not well enough to leave their homes. One man I called was blind, another sat all day, every day by the bed of his wife who could no longer remember or respond to his voice.

Those who did the most to make the demonstration a success, in spite of small numbers, are modest men. With some rare exceptions, they had not wished to denounce government policies in public, but realized time was running short and over the decades few in government had listened and most had ignored their complaints.

They weren't asking much, just equitable treatment: a medical card for instance, the kind given to service veterans; treatment and accommodation during illness, and in cases of serious need, some pension recognition. As one of our members said on August 9, Veterans Affairs Canada brags that medical and health benefits are available to us; that is true and no thanks to the bureaucrats. That was not the case in the decades between war's end and the institution of universal health care. Our comrades remember the neglect of a succession of ministers responsible for veterans affairs: Hees, Merrithew, Campbell, MacAulay et al. If I have missed a name in this line-up of shallow vessels, keep in mind they were all rich in promises and poor in positive response.

The innocent ignorance of history on the part of many reporters who questioned us on the facts of our situation is understandable. Their parents were perhaps not yet born in the years we spent at sea and any references to the wartime merchant marine received only cursory notice in the press and were almost entirely absent in Canadian schoolbooks.

"What did merchant ships do in the war, didn't the navy do everything?"

"Did you people get much higher pay than those in the Armed Forces?"

"What do you want? VAC people told us a few minutes ago that merchant seamen are eligible for the same benefits as service people."

"Why aren't there more of you demonstrating?"

"Is this the first time you've taken your complaints to people?"

Appropriate replies would have required a brief lecture on history to refute falsehoods engendered by people and agencies for selfish reasons, as well as some information on seamen still alive and now nearing their ninth decade. And yes, we have gone public and political, while the leaders representing retired Armed Forces associations opposed our right to equal recognition. The sands of time are running out.

The unkindest cut of all was in the question: "Didn't you go to sea to stay out of the Armed Forces?" That jovial inquiry came from a slim young man, who we knew could not understand the motivation of young people in the 1939-45 period. We could only think that a whole new generation had not been exposed to the realities of history, to the threat of the Axis and the near-miss of German domination over all Europe under the swastika.

In the Halifax demonstration we were confident that our elderly comrades would display their placards and voice their opinions with dignity. Some members who did not take part said they would not carry a placard and one man told me he did not believe in public posturing, adding that he thought our efforts would be better directed to the attention of politicians in the seats of power. Regrettably, in the Halifax-Dartmouth area only one or two master mariners attended or indicated support in principle. That may be to some degree a continuation of the exalted dignity some, but not all, senior officers feel is what they deserve. In other parts of Canada, and in other countries such as Australia, it is a different story. Veteran master mariners are active and supportive in the cause of recognition.

The attitude of Veterans Affairs Canada, implementing the policies of a series of governments, has been particularly odious in relation to former prisoners-of-war and amputees. One quaint provision in their situation was that a so-called vocational allowance, if it was eventually granted to a POW, would only apply if such training was marine-related and the individual under thirty years of age. It is interesting to ponder the exclusion of training for shore employment at a time when the federal government was even then contemplating the draconian reduction of our wartime merchant fleet. The merchant marine prisoner-of-war was not eligible for clothing allowance, technical or college training, and the negative list goes on.

On that sunny August day as merchant navy people gathered in cities across Canada, their numbers included striplings of seventy-five and up with some approaching their mid-eighties. But the poignant history of the merchant navy's contribution in war is highlighted by men who went to sea in their very early teens. Their stories, all verifiable, are a necessary reminder of those who served more than their obligation to a great nation required at an age when they should have been entering high school. For so many, their education, if they survived, would be in the intransigence of national and institutional policies; the contribution of merchant navy service veterans eminently forgettable to the point of deliberate neglect.

There was a surprising number of these kids, some of them still alive across the country. I can only write about those I have met, with one exception, at the Halifax demonstration. Max Zwicker of Halifax declares he is "going to be a thorn in the government side!" He lived in Liverpool on Nova Scotia's south shore and signed on a merchantman under the Canadian flag in 1940. He was fourteen. Max served as a deckhand and gunner on the ancient weapons retrieved from obsolescent storage and reinstalled on the poopdeck of most Allied merchant ships as the war progressed. He experiences frequent, strong flashbacks of ships picked off from convoys and going down. On August 12, 1996, the CBC Saturday morning radio program *The House* carried the following item:

> *Narrator:* They may have been the difference between victory and defeat in World War Two but fifty years after the fighting stopped, Canada's merchant seamen are still involved in a fight with their own government. Hundreds of merchant mariners in cities across Canada carried placards this week outside of the Department of Veterans Affairs. They were protesting

against their treatment by successive Canadian governments since World War Two.

In the war, the merchant navy was called the fourth branch of the armed services, praised by Winston Churchill among others for service on the supply ships that nourished the Allied war effort. But they were virtually ignored by the Canadian government after the war, while army, navy, and air force veterans were given access to a wide range of services.

While many of the survivors received some benefits given to veterans, others say they are still being treated as second-class citizens. Ray Aboud reports:

Ray Aboud: Halifax, Wednesday morning. A handful of men, most in their seventies, gather outside the office of the Department of Veterans Affairs. It's a quiet dignified group. They hold placards saying Canada Forgets and End Discrimination. They're merchant mariners. They sailed on ships that carried the supplies for the Allied war effort: they're men and women who have been looking for fairness from the Canadian government since the war ended."

Voices of various veterans:

"We have scars still with us, the scars that the Canadian government did not treat us as fairly as the rest of the veterans who served Canada."

"I'm looking for a Veteran's Medical Card with everything on it that I could use any time to get my prescriptions and that kind of stuff, whatever I need to make my life a little bit better."

Ray Aboud: For many merchant mariners the memories of the past begin here, in the Atlantic Ocean off Halifax. During the Second World War the harbour offered refuge from the dangers of the convoy routes where merchant ships were attacked by enemy ships, submarines, and planes and they were always outgunned. Many more merchant ships were sunk than naval vessels; 1 in 10 merchant mariners died, a higher attrition rate than the regular armed forces, but the supply lines were never broken.

Foster Griezic is an historian at Carleton University in Ottawa and an advocate for merchant mariners:

Foster Griezic: There is no doubt that without them the war couldn't have been won because the mass transportation of war materiel could not have been carried to Great Britain, to the Mediterranean, to Malta, to North Africa, to the Far East. It was the lifeline of the war.

Ray Aboud: It is impossible to overstate the hardships many merchant mariners faced, the personal sacrifices they made. When he was 17, Edison Yeadon sailed off to a war he relives in his nightmares, nightmares of three years as a prisoner of war at Kawasakai Camp #1 near Tokyo.

Edison Yeadon: I was beaten with rifle butts, and kicked and booted, and ... I got sick after that and I was sick for a good month, I guess. I had sores all up my legs, stuff like that. That's from lack of proper food. And the bed bugs could almost carry you out of the camp."

Ray Aboud: Mr. Yeadon watched other merchant seamen die in the camp. After the war on a train home to Nova Scotia, he had to borrow money from regular veterans to buy food. Merchant seamen were denied benefits other veterans got such as full compensation for time spent as prisoners of war, education, housing, and land grants, health care, and disability pensions.

A bill introduced by the Conservative government in 1992 gave them access to more benefits but set restrictions that excluded them from others.

Bill Hutcherson of Vancouver is 71 now; he was a radio operator on a merchant ship during the war.

Bill Hutcherson: You see people now that are driving trucks, mowing lawns, etc. and they put these ear protectors on their ears. We put earphones on our ears to blast noise into them. Well. I ended up with impaired hearing."

Ray Aboud: Hutcherson was denied a disability pension once, denied one again on appeal.

Bill Hutcherson: And they're indicating now they think they'll give me a five per cent pension, they think, and it only goes back to the date that I made application which was when the merchant navy were allowed to make such claims which was three years.

Ray Aboud: Many others share Bill Hutcherson's frustration. Muriel MacDonald is secretary of the Merchant Navy Coalition for Equality; her late husband was a merchant seaman. She fears the Chretien government won't remove the inequities because merchant mariners don't represent many votes.

Muriel MacDonald: There's so few survivors left, less than three thousand. That means people have little to offer politically, no political clout. I've been to standing committee hearings and it's sort of polite, benign, passive neglect.

Ray Aboud: The Centre Block, Parliament Hill, Thursday. Journalists and camera crews wait while the Liberal caucus meets in private. In opposition, the Liberals praised the contribution of Canada's merchant mariners and supported equal status for them under veterans legislation with no discrimination whatsoever.

Today, only a few are publicly taking the same position. Warren Allmand is an MP for Montreal.

Warren Allmand: I think they deserve the full rights, I mean, we went part way a few years ago, I think we should go the full way and give them all the rights of veterans.

Ray Aboud: Other countries such as the US, Australia, and Norway have a different history. They've treated their merchant seamen pretty much the same as other veterans. Canada hasn't and time is clearly running out.

Foster Griezic: If they're averaging 75 years of age right now, in five years the average will be 80 years, and they're dying off at the rate of one every three days and the rate is increasing. There is something fundamentally wrong that people in their seventies have to take to the streets to demonstrate and protest the government's inaction on the situation.

Ray Aboud: Merchant mariners are proud of their contribution to the war effort, proud of comrades who died to keep the supply lines flowing. They wear their medals with honour on Remembrance Day, but they still feel a deep anguish over the indifference of some veterans groups and successive federal governments. Some feel they'll never win equal treatment with other veterans; the government will simply wait until the last merchant mariner is gone and the last cry for equality is silenced.

Following these interviews, Secretary of State for Veterans Affairs Lawrence MacAulay was asked if it was time this inequity was corrected. He responded: "It is certainly true that they played a major part in the war effort and merchant marine veterans have a right to the same benefits and privileges as any other veteran in this country. There have been a number of complaints, but if someone can show me a case where a merchant mariner has been discriminated against because he's a merchant mariner I would like to have that evidence."

The interviewer, Alvin Cater, said that to hear Mr. MacAulay's side of it, there was absolutely no inequality in the system, "yet you have these 3,000 veterans, merchant seamen, their families or survivors saying that there is a whole host of injustices in the system. How can there be this incredible discrepancy?"

Mr. MacAulay: Alvin, I certainly would first like to say that there are over 3,000 veterans who did a lot for the war effort and I very much appreciate that as a country. But I would question if there are three thousand who are complaining about the way they are treated by the Department of Veterans Affairs and the Canadian government, I would very much question that.

Alvin Cater: Now, you've been meeting with them, you've talked with them, you've heard their complaints. Do you get the sense that they are asking for what amounts to special treatment?

Mr. MacAulay: I've met with many merchant mariners who are very pleased with the Department of Veterans Affairs and the Canadian government and also are very quick to indicate that this government has the best package or one of the best packages of benefits for veterans in the world. What we want to be sure of is that every veteran is treated fairly. And, under the present system I feel, and many other people, most people in this country, feel that all veterans are treated quite well.

Alvin Cater: Does fair treatment mean equal treatment?

Mr. MacAulay: Yes, what it means is that you have equal dollars if you are concerned about disability pensions or health allowances, yes.

Alvin Cater: Are merchant mariners free to call you?

Mr. MacAulay: Absolutely, Alvin, and I would be very pleased to talk to them at any time because I have a great appreciation for what the merchant mariners and all other veterans did for this country.

We may hope that Mr. MacAulay will be just as pleased to respond to our letters. I wrote a lengthy letter to Mr. MacAulay on May 14, 1995 and as this is written (February 1997) its receipt has not been acknowledged. It may be that his staff is examining my comments on statements he made in an earlier letter to Francis LeBlanc, MP with reference to one of Mr. LeBlanc's constituents. I await a detailed response to the questions I presented relative to merchant marine veteran status.

The significant omission in the minister's responses on the CBC Radio program is that generalities obscure the sticking point, namely, will the government compensate merchant navy veterans for the decades of neglect, for the absence of educational, employment, or minimal rehabilitation benefits at war's end and beyond?

The Chronicle-Herald of Halifax has consistently called for fair treatment of Canada's merchant marine veterans; that newspaper had and still has an intimate knowledge of the merchant navy's contribution. During the war years, managing editor Bob Rankin and his staff could frequently glance down Buckingham Street which ends at harbourside and observe a line of merchant ships out of Bedford Basin proceeding to the outer harbour and through the protective gates; once in open water the ships moved into convoy formation off Chebucto Head before disappearing into the eastward mists. The paper understood the problems and perils of shipping vast quantities of war materiel across the ocean under continuing threat of attack, in danger zones that extended from Thrumcap Shoal at the harbour's mouth to Britain's western approaches and ports of destination on the Irish Sea and other havens in the United Kingdom. From very early in the war, the paper numbered each day as another milestone in the war against Hitlerism. The publication remains closely attuned to Canada's defence posture in a city that was founded only four years after Louisbourg fell to New England forces in 1745.

On August 11, 1995, two days after merchant navy veterans demonstrated in cities across Canada, *The Chronicle-Herald* expressed its views in a muscular editorial:

Saying thanks decades too late

Hostilities formally ceased fifty years ago, but Canada's merchant marine veterans understandably feel like they're still fighting a war.

Their war, however, is not with any foreign enemy, but with what they perceive is an ungrateful nation, and an uncaring federal bureaucracy, out to deny them equal treatment with regular armed forces veterans.

"We'd be much better received if we had been a Japanese internee or a former U-boat crew member returning for a visit," complained Doug Fraser Thursday, a day after he and fellow veterans staged nationwide demonstrations to again bring their long-standing complaints to public light.

Canada's merchant seamen were, indeed, treated much differently than regular veterans at war's end.

It's only in recent years that the federal government began to right the decades old wrongs, first by changing the law books, and second by awarding medals commemorating their role in wartime.

Their mistreatment is easily documented. For starters, they were denied rehabilitation grants, free university education, land grants, and job preference provided veterans of the armed forces.

That's why ex-seamen are demanding retroactive payment — in the range of $20,000 each – to compensate for lost benefits.

A Veterans Affairs spokesperson in Ottawa says such benefits are no longer on the books, adding that making such a payment is now strictly a political question that's out of DVA's hands.

Although ex-sailors make a valid case of unfair treatment, it would not be practical, feasible or prudent to grant the estimated 3,000 surviving merchant mariners retroactive cheques. It would not only be costly, but set a precedent for a host of similar retroactive claims.

The priority should be placed, instead, on making sure surviving merchant mariners have equal access to health programs long available to regular armed forces veterans.

Ottawa took a major, and long overdue step in 1992 when the Department of Veterans Affairs first recognized the civilian sailors as veterans. That made survivors eligible for pensions and other benefits. DVA says two-thirds of the estimated 3,000 survivors now receive some benefits.

But those ex-mariners hitting the streets this week complain they are not getting a fair shake and argue they fall under a complex parliamentary act with cross-references to seven acts and regulations with 40 major exclusions to equality.

Ironically, DVA says it received its first formal case seeking review of eligible benefits only this week. (Aug. 6-11, 1995)

Canada's program of benefits for Armed Forces veterans was and is fair and comprehensive, if not generous. How else could one consider acceptance of a nine-mile ferry voyage from Cape Tormentine, New Brunswick to Borden, Prince Edward Island as qualification for overseas service. Conversely, those who served in the Canadian merchant marine have not been granted equal recognition as veterans of war in spite of praiseworthy comments from many and various sources in a position to understand the dangers and a percentage of loss much higher than for the three Armed Forces.

The ranks of merchant mariners who served in the Second World War are thinning, yet some of us plan to live for a good long time yet and will continue to fight for deserved recognition. We may not win equal status and reasonable compensation, however, our epitaph will endure:

ENSE ET ARATO

Serving in war and in peace.